FROM THE DUST

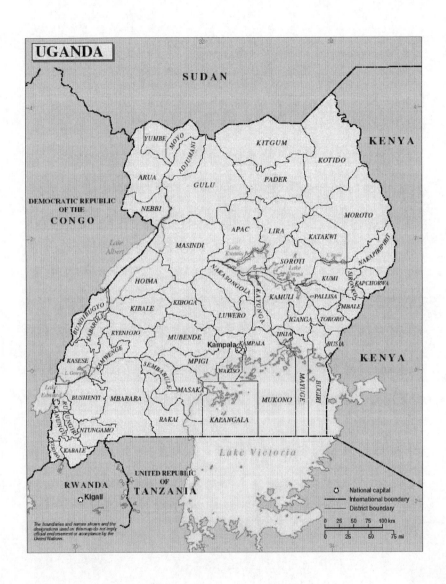

From the Dust

A *Sequel to* A Distant Grief

F. KEFA SEMPANGI
with JENNIFER MELVIN

WIPF *&* STOCK · Eugene, Oregon

FROM THE DUST
A Sequel to *A Distant Grief*

www.wipfandstock.com

ISBN 13: 978-1-55635-561-5

Manufactured in the U.S.A.

From the Dust is dedicated to the memory of Mrs. Anky Rookmaaker, wife of my former professor Hans Rookmaaker of Vrie University, Amsterdam. Mrs. Rookmaaker's encouragement and support led me to begin the children's work in Uganda. Her love, simplicity, commitment, and dedication to working with the needy peoples of Uganda, Kenya, Ethiopia, and India have made the world a better place.

Contents

The Moshi Spirit

SOWING IN TEARS

"**D**ADDY, LISTEN!" CALLED MY daughter, Damali, suddenly interrupting the casual conversation around the lunch table. "Amin is on the run! The Tanzanian army has attacked Uganda!" Our eyes turned quickly to the news broadcast coming from the nearby television. Suddenly my body became numb and my mouth became as dry as that of a man facing a roaring lion.

Just the mention of the name *Idi Amin* stirred emotions in me that are inexplicable in any language. Amin was the tyrant responsible for thousands of deaths of friends and fellow Ugandans, the brutal slaughter of innocent citizens, and the senseless genocide of precious souls. As the president of Uganda and a truly demonic individual, Amin had led a rampage, killing anyone whom he suspected of opposing him or anyone who could possibly have ever considered opposing him. Although I had seemingly been immune to his wrath for years, suddenly and without cause I had become his number-one target. Perhaps his wrath was directed at me because so many were coming to Christ through the ministry of the church I pastored, the Redeemed Church; but for whatever reason, he had forced me into fleeing the country, separating me from my relatives, friends, and church.

My exile began in 1973. My family and I had just spent four months in Amsterdam. I had been working on my doctorate at the Free University, and we were developing a lasting and deep relationship with one of my professors, Dr. Rookmaaker, and his wife Anky. The Rookmaakers were deeply committed Christians who took me in as their son and greatly influenced my life for Christ. Those were wonderful days of learning and growing, but by the end of the summer, we were eager to return to Uganda, to our friends and family, and to our work there with the Redeemed Church and the Kijomanyi Children's Home. Despite several vague telegrams from home warning us to stay in Amsterdam, we were determined to return. But before we left, our friends gave us a warm farewell party, and at the end of the evening, Mrs. Rookmaaker handed us two "safety" airplane tickets from Uganda to Amsterdam, just in case we needed them. We were sure we wouldn't, but tucked them away hoping to use them to send two Ugandan young people to the university in Amsterdam to study.

Arriving at the Entebbe airport in Uganda, we were shocked to be met by one of Amin's former assassins. This Nubian (member of a tribe of warriors who were known for raiding and killing) had come to our church on the previous Easter Sunday with four of his fellow assassins to kill me. With their guns pointed at my head, they had given me one last opportunity to speak before I died. Not realizing that it was I who was speaking, I heard the words of surrender to God's will coming from my mouth. I told them that I would pray that after my death God would have mercy on them and spare them from eternal destruction. To my surprise, one of them asked that I pray for them. I did, and they suddenly lowered their guns and left. Amazingly, in subsequent days each one of them came to a commitment to Jesus Christ.

Now, my wife, Penina, and I, along with our baby daughter, Damali, were being whisked through the airport by this formidable man. Should we trust him? I wondered. Had he truly been converted, or had his decision to trust Christ been a trick? He shoved us into an unfamiliar car driven by another man in disguise. Questions flooded my mind. Was I leading my family to our death by trusting these men?

Our driver turned out to be a trusted friend. He drove us to a safe house where we were able to visit with friends, relatives, and elders of the Redeemed Church throughout the night and finally to get some rest and food. We were informed that my name was at the top of Amin's list of wanted men and that just days before, he had arrested and tortured many of our church elders in hopes of obtaining information of my whereabouts. This home was to be a temporary safe house until they could locate a more permanent hiding place for us. However, soon after we awoke the following day, we learned that Amin had been informed of our location, and that we had just minutes to escape. We gathered one suitcase of belongings and were driven several miles to a bus park where we boarded a worker bus bound for Nairobi.

Crossing the border from Uganda to Kenya was a terrifying experience. Five hundred of our six hundred shillings were confiscated, and our lives were threatened. When we finally arrived in Nairobi, we spent the day walking the streets searching for friends we knew. Unable to locate even one acquaintance, we were forced to spend ninety shillings on a room and breakfast.

The following morning as we were eating, Penina noticed a Nubian at the motel desk, and as we listened, we realized he was looking for me. We quickly grabbed our suitcase and the baby, hurried out the back door, and began running. We both realized that if the State Research Bureau were still looking for us, even in Nairobi, it would not be long until they found us. We were not safe there and needed to return to Amsterdam immediately.

We found a stranger on the street, who was willing to drive us to the airport, and who refused to take any money for the trip. His wife even gave us ten shillings to tip the porter! Fortunately the porter refused the tip, and our last twenty shillings were used to pay the airline clearance tax.

Soon we were safely in the air but without money, home, country, possessions, a job, visas, or entrance papers. Our dreams were destroyed, our friends were still in danger, and we were overwhelmed with grief. But the last words of my dear friend Dr. Kibaya to me that night in the "safe house" were ringing in my ears: "The whole world might turn against you," he had reminded me. "But Jesus Christ stands with you." Jesus Christ was standing with us. We could so clearly see how he had directed our footsteps and brought us through the hurricane. He had provided escape for us not just once, but three times. He had provided money and airline tickets when we had needed them. If he had not let us down so far, why should we worry now? Surely he would see us through whatever storms remained. Certainly his grace was sufficient, and his strength would be made perfect in our weakness!

The next storm came when we landed at Schiphol International Airport just outside of Amsterdam. The customs officers had no compassion on any traveler without documents. We told our story repeatedly but to no avail. They refused to believe such a wild tale and treated us as if we were criminals. We begged them to call the Free University to verify our story, but our pleas were ignored. Their only option, they said, was to put us on a plane back to Uganda. It seemed as if our world were crashing in around us, and we were helpless. Returning to Uganda meant certain death. Had they no compassion for our situation?

Finally a government investigator entered the room and, after a thorough inquiry into our situation, agreed to contact the university. An hour later Dr. Rookmaaker and Dr. Van Noord, a high-ranking official from the university, arrived on the scene and were able to convince the authorities to extend sanctuary to us and protect us from "Uganda's Hitler." Six hours after our landing, we were given temporary identification papers and released.

Although we were out of Uganda, we were not necessarily safe. We began to hear reports of the assassination and terrorizing of Ugandans in exile in France and England. One evening while shopping, Penina was severely frightened by a dark muscular man with Nubian tribal scars, staring at her as if he were stalking her. Reports began to come to us from friends left in Uganda indicating the worsening situation there. My friend Ali wrote that just thirty minutes after we had crossed the border into Kenya, the borders had been closed in an effort to trap us. Amin's agents had traced us to Nairobi and then to the airport, but only after we had been airborne for thirty minutes. The Redeemed Church had been closed, and members of the congregation were meeting in private homes for worship. Our house had been completely plundered, and our car was being driven by a well-known army captain. Two men who were in charge of the Kijomanyi Children's Home had had to flee for their lives, the orphanage had been closed, and the children had been turned out onto the streets.

The hardest blow came with the news of the capture and torturous death of my dear brother in Christ, Kiwanuka. Amin himself had beaten him to death with a sledgehammer, had performed blood rituals over his remains, and then cut off his head and stored it in his freezer. Kiwanuka had died a martyr's death, praying for the forgiveness of his murderer's sins and calling on the name of Jesus as he died at Amin's feet.

My grief over Kiwanuka's passing was overwhelming. I lost all hope for the future of Uganda and the ministries there. All we had prayed and worked for was now gone. I cried out, "Oh, God, where are you?"

His answer came quickly as he brought to my mind the words of an elderly woman just after the death of another dear friend: "You know," she had said to me, "through many losses of family and friends and through much sorrow, the Lord has taught me one thing. Jesus Christ did not come to take away our pain and suffering, but to share in it."

Almost a year later, the gentle words of the woman took on new meaning. God was not mourning over his people from a distance. His own Son had suffered the defeat of physical pain and death and still suffered with his suffering children. We did not weep alone; Jesus Christ wept with us. But our sadness was only for a season: "He that goeth forth and weepeth, bearing precious seed, shall doubtless come again with rejoicing, bringing his sheaves with him" (Ps 126:6). What Kiwanuka and thousands of other martyrs had sown in tears, they and the church with them would reap in joy.

In February of 1974, Penina, Damali, and I said goodbye to our friends in Holland and boarded a plane for the United States. We flew to Philadelphia where I began a three-year program of theological studies at Westminster Seminary and later began the Africa Foundation. Through the foundation we were able to give aid to Ugandan refugees who were suffering in Kenya, unable to work or go to school, and who were living in desperate conditions due to strict Kenyan laws forbidding refugees from holding jobs. As we reached out to the suffering refugees, we realized that the story did not end with Amin. We came to understand that what Amin had meant for evil, God had meant for good. For every story of atrocities and death, there was another story that went unreported and unnoticed. It was the story of those who, by faith, had "escaped the edge of the sword" (Heb 11:34), and of those who, by faith, "were slain with the sword" (Heb 11:37). It was the story of how God's people in the midst of great suffering had come to understand the depths of love. And it was the story of how God, in his providence, had led his children into the wilderness to prepare a table for them.

THE MOSHI CONFERENCE

For six years we labored in America, waiting with hope for the day that Amin would be defeated and expelled from power. And now it looked as if that day had come. I was hypnotized by that small flash of news, and in my daze I envisioned myself landing at the Entebbe airport with a big welcome of hallelujahs from our friends and church members. My heart beat wildly at the thought of my beloved country's being freed from tyranny and of my family and me, along with thousands of other refugees, returning to the life we had once known.

"Daddy, we will get a full picture at the prime news," insisted Damali, and we anxiously began the wait for more information as questions whirled in our minds. However, before the news broadcast came, there was a telephone call from New York. It was from Namakajo, calling on behalf of the organizing chairman of our pressure group, Godfrey Binaisa Lukongwa. A conference was to be held in Moshi, a small town in northern Tanzania, and the Africa Foundation had been invited to send three delegates. The purpose of the conference was twofold: to elect a government in exile and to present the appearance that it was the disgruntled Ugandans fighting to live in their own country who were attempting to overthrow Amin rather than the Tanzanian government. The foundation had to immediately provide three travel tickets for Binaisa, Luyimbazi Zake, and me. It was wise, of course, at this point to leave my family in the security of America, awaiting either my return or my call to them to join me when it was safe for them to reenter Uganda.

When we arrived in Moshi, we found that Namakajo had gone ahead of us and was among the American journalists, so we hired a taxi from the airport. This particular taxi, with a roof patched with metal pieces, was a sign of poverty in the region. But that did not shock anyone, as it was better than even the affluence of the exiles' lives. Traveling to the location of the conference was further complicated by the notorious checkpoints along the way, which were manned by soldiers and militia.

The conference was an exciting time as we laid the foundation for the new day that was dawning in Uganda. A democratic spirit was born in those days in March of 1979. Before any names were considered for nomination to leadership, Dr. Aliker had proposed that only men of substance be considered. Yusufu Lule was unanimously elected as a man of substance to serve as the new president. In addition, we adopted four cardinal principles that we vowed to implement: unity, democracy, national independence, and social progress. We established our imminent government objectives to be political acceptability, accommodation, and reconciliation; and with these ideas, we planned to forge a coherent national unity and to live in harmony with one another. With our new government officials elected and foundational principles established, we eagerly awaited the final deposition of Idi Amin in order to return home and begin restoration.

By May of 1979, Amin had been removed, the Liberation War was over, and it was safe for us to return to Uganda. The executive members who had been chosen in Moshi formed the cabinet and in June 1979, president Lule led the first National Consultative Council (NCC) meeting in the Nile Conference Center in Kampala. After only sixty days in office, Lule was removed and replaced by Godfrey Binaisa. At the same time, I was appointed deputy minister in charge of rehabilitation. What a perfect position for me to be able to serve my fellow countrymen and to open doors of ministry to spread the gospel! How marvelous is the hand of God!

At first only we *returnees*, as we who had left were called, were permitted to hold government positions, but in October changes were made that allowed the *stayees* to be included. A committee was formed to interview people from all around the country who had applied to join the NCC. When I was elected chairman of that committee, I made certain that the *stayees* were also granted opportunity to serve in government positions.

My mind was not prepared to accept the devastation I would find when I returned to my country. I soon discovered what a tremendous job was before us to rebuild a destroyed country and to bring healing to shattered lives. I felt as Nehemiah must have felt when he returned to Jerusalem to rebuild the crumbled walls. The shame of the city's lying in waste spurred him into action, and as he surveyed the ruins by night, he determined to be a catalyst among the people to accomplish the work and will of God. As he challenged the people, he reminded them that the hand of God was upon him, and it would be through God's strength and power that the task would be accomplished. Even in the face of resistance in the form of laughter and scorn, Nehemiah trusted in God's strength. He proclaimed, "The God of heaven, he will prosper us; therefore we his servants will arise and build" (Neh 2:20b).

2

The Homecoming

THE WELCOME

ARRIVING AT ENTEBBE AIRPORT was the most emotional experience of my life. My first sight was a bright banner that read, "Entebbe Airport Welcomes You!" I indeed felt welcome. The sunshine was warm and homey, and even the bullet-ridden buildings of the airport seemed to force a smile at me. I spontaneously waved hello to the airport porters, and as they waved back, I felt myself in the grasp of the traditional Ugandan warm-heartedness. It was good to be home.

As I drove from Entebbe to Kampala, I gazed at the trees with their luscious green foliage stretching to the green hills in the horizon. I stared at the infinite expanse of Lake Nalubale (Lake Victoria). As we passed another cluster of trees, I saw in the distance three black monkeys (one with a baby clinging to her back) excitedly chasing one another from branch to branch. Brightly colored weaverbirds chirped loudly, flapping their yellow wings in the sunshine. I smelled the natural fragrances of my country and felt a great peace descending upon me.

In Kampala, like other government officials, I was booked into the former Apollo Hotel, but now ironically named the International Hotel. It was in a sorry state. The remains of campfires were on the driveway and on the verandas. Rotten garbage dumps were heaped here and there. The walls were coated with dirt, and dust was everywhere. At the hotel reception desk, I was given the room key, which opened the door only with great difficulty, as the locks were faulty. I was longing for a shower after my long journey, but when I turned on the tap in the bathroom, I heard the whistle of an airlock and received only a small trickle of water, barely enough to wet my hands. "Well, so much for a shower," I thought and then walked over to the window. From the thirteenth floor, I felt the cool breeze traveling from Lake Nalubale and caressing my face.

According to the paper that I had picked up at the reception desk, government business was to commence in four days, led by those of us who had been at the Moshi conference. I had time to sleep and clear off much of the jet lag.

After a good rest and lunch, I decided to go for a stroll. I was not really sure whether it was wise to venture out of the hotel confines, but since the liberation guards were deployed at every corner of the city, I decided to take the chance. I was appalled at the sights I saw. Most of the buildings were in ruins. The few remaining ones stood abandoned and lifeless, like men without eyes.

I walked along Kampala Road toward the Central Bank of Uganda. Opposite the bank had stood the largest supermarket in Kampala, where we used to go on Saturdays for shopping. Now there were half walls and rubble. The Liberation War had come like a violent storm, sweeping everything in its path and leaving the city empty and barren.

I headed down to Market Street. From a distance, I saw commotion and scuffles in the large space near the market. Approaching the crowd, I saw a man stripped naked in the grip of what looked like mob justice. The Tanzanian soldiers were speaking to the man in Swahili, and from the conversation of those around me, I learned that this man had served in Amin's army and had stripped to disguise himself as a lunatic. The "disguise" did not fool anyone, and he found himself standing naked before the people he had once bullied, mistreated, and terrorized, having to beg for their mercy. The people were teasing him, kicking him in the back, and screaming, "Shoot him, shoot him!"

The Tanzanian soldiers took the culprit away, preventing the mob from taking revenge. As the Land Rover drove away with him, the crowd dispersed, disgruntled by the decision of the soldiers but voicing their disapproval rather quietly, fearful that they might offend the liberators.

I made my way down into the Nakasero Market. After the Liberation War, the markets had become the most crowded places in Kampala. Most essential commodities like soap, sugar, matches, and salt were available only in markets. The shops were literally empty due to massive looting. The market vendors had helped themselves to all the goods in the shops and were now selling them from market stalls at incredibly low prices. The goods, which had been available only to the rich, had now been made available to the venders at no cost by what they thought was President Lule's Liberation War. Commodities were reduced from the sky-scraping prices of Amin's reign to the rock-bottom prices that they called "little prices." The price of a kilo of sugar is a good example. Under Amin it cost two hundred shillings, and now it was selling for only fifty shillings. Beef had sold for three hundred shillings per kilo, and now it was only half that price.

THE GOSPEL BEGINS TO SPREAD

My third day in the country brought another big surprise. One of my closest associates in the work of the gospel prior to my escape, Joseph Musitwa, had spread the word that the man who had preached the gospel in defiance of Amin's order was back in the country. Joseph, along with several other pastors of the Redeemed Church, had raised the money to rent a hall along Nasser Road. The believers gave me a rousing welcome, and many turned out to hear the gospel and to be healed of their diseases and to have their demons cast out.

The meeting gave me the opportunity to share my new mission and to tell the story of my escape. I spelled out my new ambitions: to reactivate my work with homeless street children, to establish a Reformed community in Uganda, and to participate in the political vanguard. I closed the meeting by calling upon all charismatic pastors from the faith churches to have their theology revolutionized through discipleship. I was eager to disciple them in the Reformed theology that I had had the privilege of embracing while studying in America. This invitation did not augur well with many pastors who were now self-styled apostles and prophets of the sort.

I rented a hall in the International Hotel, but only thirty-five pastors showed up for the first meeting. Soon we moved the meeting to the Nile Hotel, but the number of the faithful students had reduced to ten. Finally we moved to my hotel room, where I had the opportunity to teach the ten points of Calvinism in depth to men like Joseph Musitwa, Pastor Sozi, Edward Kasaija, Kintu, and Pastor Nkata. The men were eager to learn, and our meetings would go on beyond midnight.

For many of the believers, the Reformed faith was a landmark in their understanding of Christianity and of the Scriptures. Some Christians had gone as far as thinking that every time they heard a good sermon, they could be born again. According to their misconception, a person could be born again several times in his lifetime. Also there was little understanding of the differences between justification and sanctification. I labored to explain that while justification and regeneration were once and for all, sanctification was a continuous process. Regeneration was the new birth, but once a child was born into the family of God, there was the Christian life to be lived. Through sanctification, a baby Christian grows in his relationship with the Savior and daily becomes more like Christ in his actions and attitudes. Regeneration could not overshadow other stages of development in the Christian life.

Time and time again, I had to explain that salvation was a unity covering the three stages of justification, sanctification, and glorification. "Faith evangelism" had twisted Ephesians 2:8, "For by grace are ye saved, through faith, and that not of yourselves, it is the gift of God." I had to use several examples to illustrate that while we are saved through faith, the basis of our salvation is not our own faith but the finished work of our Lord Jesus Christ on the cross. Faith is believing that finished work.

Another difficult idea to explain to charismatic pastors was that miracles do not qualify a person to be a Christian. This teaching was hard to swallow for pastors whose preaching depended on their performance as miracle workers. Our Lord described John the Baptist as a great prophet in Luke 7:28: "For I say unto you, Among those that are born of women there is not a greater prophet than John the Baptist." But in John 10:41, the Apostle John wrote of John the Baptist as having the reputation of a man who did no miracles. The pastors needed to come to grips with the truths that miracles do not qualify a person as a prophet, and that a pastor need not perform miracles to validate his ministry.

In response to my explanation, one pastor said to me, "Kefa, I don't know anybody who has cast out more demons than you have. You know the nature of our people. Do you really expect me to keep anybody in my congregation without my performing miracles?" That pastor never returned to my discipleship classes.

I was so excited to share all that I had learned at Westminster Seminary. In my first weeks at the college, I had had no problem accepting the doctrines of man's total depravity and God's unconditional love towards a sinner. Many times one of our pastors or teachers would assign a doctrinal book for us to read, and then we would meet and discuss the book. This was a method that I used with my group of students. How God worked through that group! Edward Kasajja and Peterson Sozi went to America to study, and later John Ntale and Baker Katende joined them. Emmie Mulondo and Emma Kiwanuka were offered scholarships to the Reformed Bible College in Grand Rapids, and Emma was able to continue studies for a master's degree at Westminster Seminary in Escondido. Joseph Musitwa went to Australia to study. These men who were first involved in the theology study group returned from abroad fired up with the Reformed faith. They taught others and confirmed to them that I was speaking "true theology," and that Presbyterianism was indeed a dominant force in America, Canada, and Australia. What a thrill it was for me to converse with like-minded brethren as their eyes of understanding had been opened! These brethren were strengthened to start churches in Mbale, Kampala, Fort Portal, and Luwero.

The spread of the gospel throughout our ravaged country was a marvelous testimony to the powerful work of the Holy Spirit. Such widespread church planting could never have been accomplished in man's strength. I was so honored that God had allowed me to play even a small role in the founding of the Presbyterian Church in Uganda. I was careful to make it clear that, although I was called the founder, I was certainly not the foundation. The foundation is Jesus Christ, and to him be the glory.

> Therefore thus saith the Lord GOD, Behold, I lay in Zion for a foundation a stone, a tried stone, a precious corner stone, a sure foundation: he that believeth shall not make haste. (Isa 28:16)

> For other foundation can no man lay than that is laid, which is Jesus Christ. (1 Cor 3:11)

GARBAGE EVANGELISM

Two Americans came to Uganda that first year and had a very positive impact for the gospel. Jack Miller and Harvey Conn were two of my professors at Westminster Seminary. Jack taught evangelism and Harvey taught missions. Jack did not hesitate to launch an evangelistic crusade in Old Kampala, but the meetings were not very successful. Harvey, on the other hand, came up with a more creative way of reaching the people with the gospel. He had taken a walk in the short streets of Old Kampala and was shocked that everywhere he turned, he saw huge, stinking mounds of garbage. As he gazed at these garbage dumps, he thought of a strategic plan for evangelism.

In the evening evangelistic meeting, Harvey asked whether it was possible to get shovels and a garbage truck from the City Council. By ten o'clock the following day, the garbage truck was parked outside the students' residence. Right away Jack Miller, Harvey Conn, and the students they had brought from the seminary began shoveling garbage in our immediate neighborhood along Namirembe Road.

For nine years people had not seen a white man, for Amin had expelled both the whites and Asians at the same time. It was a spectacular sight to see white men shoveling garbage and making the city clean. This scene attracted a huge crowd to the extent that some climbed on top of the tall buildings to have a clear view of this rare occurrence. The people could hardly believe what they were seeing. An old woman was heard thanking God for enabling her to live long enough to witness this spectacular event.

The work continued until four thirty in the afternoon. After the truck had made several trips to dump its loads, the professors were ready to climb the platform and preach the gospel to a bewildered crowd. The people were ready to listen to these amazing white men who had humbled themselves to labor so hard to clean up their garbage. The preachers had earned themselves a hearing, for they had fully identified with the general public.

We called this method "garbage evangelism." Later Harvey Conn held a session with the students and explained the lesson that we all had learned that day. Preaching the gospel sometimes involves getting our hands dirty. It could involve touching mud, mixing clay, and anointing the eyes of a blind man with it, just as our Lord Jesus Christ had demonstrated. Harvey warned the students not to use hygienic methods only, but to realize that, sometimes, unhygienic methods can yield more far-reaching results. Our "garbage evangelism" had made a powerful impact on the people, and many lives were transformed because of our willingness to humble ourselves.

> To the weak became I as weak, that I might gain the weak: I am made all things to all men, that I might by all means save some. (1 Cor 9:22)

3

Nakafero

IT WAS ON A certain Friday in the month of June 1979 that the parliamentary proceedings had been long and tiring. I returned to the hotel fairly exhausted. Just as I was approaching the main entrance, I heard a female voice calling my name, but I could not tell from which direction the voice was coming. Down at the main gate I spied a bit of commotion. A woman was trying to fight her way through the barricade of Tanzanian soldiers who were standing guard. I heard her voice ring out: "*Munange, munange, nyamba!*" ("My friend, my friend, help!") Suddenly I realized that the woman was Nakafero.

Memories of "the fugitive woman" flooded my mind. It was Nakafero and her desperate situation that had first motivated me to minister to the street children of Uganda, and it was her three tiny girls who had been the first children I had rescued. A local mission had used a picture of her and her children in their abject poverty to plead for assistance across America and Canada. I had personally seen the pictures in my travels and had felt compassion for them. I had also seen piles of donated clothing and supplies given to meet the needs of the poor. Later, I had met her still dressed in the same rags she had been wearing in the pictures. Angered that her situation was used to garner goods from which she received no benefit, I had determined to make a difference in her life and in the lives of others in like desperate circumstances. With the help of the Dutch organization Stitching: Save a Child, we were able to open our first orphanage, Kijomanyi Foundation Children's Home, in Kampala, and soon we were providing food, clothing, shelter, and education for Nakafero's children, as well as to hundreds like them. And now, after my long exile, I again met the woman whose life had so altered my own so many years before.

I moved quickly to rescue her from the soldiers who were restraining her. How shocked I was to see her miserable condition! She was dressed in rags, her feet were badly swollen, her neck was twisted with a mild goiter, and she was covered with dirt. As we walked together into the hotel lounge, she kept on saying, "*Ndaba kuki!*" ("Whom do I see!")

The lounge was filled with diplomats, international journalists, and fellow parliamentarians. By the time I walked through to get my room key from the reception desk, Nakafero had found herself a comfortable place to sit—she had squatted in a corner!

I spoke gently to Nakafero: "I am amazed you are still alive!" But she just continued to welcome me. Her face lit with joy despite the fact that she looked sickly and rugged.

"When you left this country, I died," she continued. "And my children, Namusisi and Norah, are at the point of starvation. They are in rags, and Topista—," she hesitated, "Topista is pregnant. You won't recognize them, orphans whom you had made clean, healthy, and in school are now the shabbiest children in town. I and my children are with hundreds of street children. We eat the scraps from the garbage dump, and our shelter is the garbage dump because it is warmer at night. The dump is a burial place, but it is the only source of income for us."

There was no way to interrupt Nakafero's outpouring of troubles. I did not blame her, for we had not seen each other for years.

"I am not worried," she continued, "now that you have returned. I no longer fear death. When I die, my children will be in your hands. Before you went into exile, I called you my son. Now I call you my father."

Nakafero's voice rose, complaining that for three weeks she had been coming to parliament and to the hotel, but nobody would let her in. She had so much to tell that I led her to my room to hear the rest.

As we entered the elevator, Nakafero's face registered fear, and as we began to go up, she sat down on the floor. I told her that there was no need for her to sit, but she prudently answered, "If the machine is moving, what is the need to remain standing?" The people in the elevator with us wanted to know what the woman had said so I explained.

There was great laughter among them all, and then the high commissioner from Cuba returned, "The woman is smarter than all of us!"

In a subdued voice Nakafero retorted: "You can laugh. Yes, I have made you laugh, but without laughter, we could not have survived Amin's repressive regime. People like me, we are left with nothing except laughter. Amin reduced us to nothing for he took everything away."

When we got into my room, Nakafero offered a prayer. Then, wiping her tears with the palm of her hand, she started to unwrap a small parcel that contained eggs. There were five of them, tiny and soiled. One of the eggs was stained with blood. She began to place the eggs in my hands, one by one, and with each egg I could feel the warmth and intensity of her love. It was as if she were saying, "I love you as I love myself." Suddenly the sense of my own importance vanished. This old woman was like my mother. In her I saw thousands of aged women living in a world that had been torn asunder by absolute poverty. I felt ashamed because I had judged her by my sophisticated, educated standards. I turned and listened to her. As she placed the last bloodstained egg in my hand, she spoke words that left tears in my eyes and in my heart.

"This small egg—dirty, tiny, and bloody—is a symbol of us, your parents, whom you left in this country. We have been famished. This blood is a symbol of Amin's regime. Animals, birds, plants, roads, buildings, and all the people bear the mark of Amin's demonic regime. It came to steal, to kill, and to destroy. But this tiny, dirty, and bloody egg has inside it life. So inside us—the dirty, skinny, and aged—is God-given life."

I took another look at Nakafero, this time with tears streaming down my face. Her face, which a few moments earlier had been covered with dust, was now filled with wisdom. In a few sentences this poor woman had summarized the history of Amin's brutal rule. Poverty and misery had taught Nakafero the philosophy of life. There was still human spirit in my country.

The following day I visited the Shauri Yako Market where Nakafero worked. She was seated in the noisiest place. She and several other women were selling wrapping paper that they had gathered out of the garbage heaps in the city. As I approached them, her children had already seen me. The three jubilant girls came running toward me, and Namusisi and Nora threw their arms around me, but Topista hung back, reluctant and shy. As the children continued their greetings, there were shouts of warning from others in the marketplace: "Keep a distance. Those are *bayaye* (street urchins)." Of course, I ignored the shouts, as I saw these girls as precious children whom I loved and whom Jesus loved. I had once cared for them in the Kijomanyi Children's Home so why should I be repulsed by them now?

As I moved toward Topista to shake her hand, Nora, the most talkative, volunteered the information. "You know, Daddy, Topista is pregnant."

A woman nearby sarcastically and with great laughter shouted, "And another *muyaye* [singular of *bayaye*] will soon be born!"

Topista stood scared and condemned, but I consoled her, assuring her that it was not wrong to bear a child. In tears she said, "Sorry, Daddy, I did not intend to let you down!"

I looked at Topista and her sisters and wondered how anyone could retain a sense of sanity in such an environment. I knew that I had to help. I could not turn my back on those whom I had loved. If I didn't help them, who would?

> Pure religion and undefiled before God and the Father is this, To visit the fatherless and widows in their affliction, and to keep himself unspotted from the world. (Jas 1:27)

4

Rohana Club

OUR FIRST CHILDREN'S HOME

THE NEWS OF IDI Amin's downfall electrified the country with enthusiasm and optimism. The people were rejoicing and relieved at the same time. Those of the diaspora especially celebrated, as it meant their freedom to return home. Journalists from around the globe converged on Uganda's capital, Kampala.

However, optimism among Ugandans was blown out of proportion. Members of the Uganda National Consultative Council (NCC) who took over the reins of power thought they could rebuild the nation in a matter of months, but they were soon to realize that the task of rebuilding the country from shambles would not be as easy as they had anticipated.

The returnees, as we who had left and now had been restored to our homeland were called, were actually endowed with a myriad of constructive ideas and an array of political theories and policies that we had collected from abroad. Even the stayees who later joined the enlarged NCC were not free from political idealism.

Before the coup, the Africa Foundation in America had commissioned over ten volunteers to go to Kenya to provide relief and counseling for many of the Ugandan refugees. Dan Herron led the team, most of whom were members of New Life Church in Philadelphia, the church in which I had served as an elder, but we also had volunteers from other states. Sarah Cox, a hard-working lady from Mississippi, recruited a number of the volunteers, among whom was George Hansburg, also from Mississippi.

Several other Christians wanted to go with me to Uganda. It was, however, not advisable to invite people to a country where pockets of

Amin's soldiers were still rampant. Nevertheless Sarah Cox and George Hansburg insisted on joining me. Sarah and George, along with George's wife and daughter, arrived in Uganda on a bus from Nairobi. They worked tirelessly with the Africa Foundation. George and another volunteer, Allan Smith, were so generous to handle all our correspondence without so much as an office. They kept track of the donors and kept our friends in Europe, Canada, and the United States informed as to the progress of the rebuilding efforts.

After my encounter with Nakafero, I was overwhelmed with the burden to once again help Kampala street children. Families had been destroyed, and the innocent children of slaughtered parents were aimlessly wandering the streets, wallowing in penury, and suffering the ravages of the cruel street life. They needed to be rescued, and Africa Foundation was the group to meet their needs.

The first task was to find a place for the home. After much searching, Sarah eventually found the perfect place in an area of Kampala called Namirembe. We were able to convince the Custodian Board to allocate the Rohana Club on Namirembe Road to the Africa Foundation, and there we began our first children's refuge.

George and his family, along with Sarah, were able to rent Mulira's house at Bakuli, which was near Namirembe. Mulira and his family had vacated their house for fear of the insecurity in the city. They had left their three fierce dogs under the care of the new tenants; but to further protect the Americans, two members of my discipleship group, Dan Situka and Baker Katende, also took up residence in the house.

Probably the biggest task we had was fighting off frustration. George was working diligently on the Rohana Club to prepare it as a suitable home for our street children. The frustration came not from a lack of funds but from the fact that there was no place in Kampala to buy the materials he needed. He could not find so much as a hinge to repair a door. We were forced to travel all the way to Nairobi, Kenya, to buy soap, toothpaste, razor blades, writing tablets, pens, shoe polish, sheets, blankets, and cooking utensils because the shops in Kampala were virtually empty, having been looted or even destroyed completely. Almost everything we needed had to be purchased in Kenya.

Having secured a location for our children's home, I realized that the next step was to gather up some children from the streets. Nakafero and her children had told me endless stories about the b*ayaye*, or street children. They knew all the places these street children slept—in cardboard boxes, in abandoned cars, on verandas, and in public restrooms. I learned later that the children who ended up in markets as *bayaye* came from different backgrounds. Many of them had seen their parents killed in cold blood. Some came from broken homes, and others had deserted their families, having been encouraged to participate in the activities of the black market. Some were inevitable victims of the Liberation War.

TAR BOY

In the first week of June 1979, I went to Owino Market. I entered by a side entrance near Nakivubo Settlement School. On the left was a sewage stream, and on either side a market wall. There were people urinating in public, and there was human excrement everywhere. I saw three dead cats, a dead dog, and stinking garbage everywhere. Several small children were playing with a dunghill insect. I walked up to the children and introduced myself. I told them I was starting a home where young boys and girls of their age could live and be taught such things as driving, mechanics, and television and radio repair, but they showed no interest. I told them that the educational programs were short, would not take long, and were free. I explained that the home would provide them with free clothing, bedding, medical care, food, and shelter.

It was difficult to hold their attention for long. These children were fidgety and competitive. They were constantly on the lookout for customers who wanted their services. Most of them were about twelve years old. Some were working as beasts of burden; others sold anything they could get their hands on. Before they wandered off, I managed to tell them that anybody who was interested could meet me at the Rohana Club on the next Thursday.

I entered into the heart of the market. The place was crowded, busy, and noisy. I noticed a boy seated on a plank of wood talking to himself. He was holding some tar in his hands and was wearing a small loincloth stained with tar. He had smeared his hair with this same tar and had drawn strange shapes on his body with it. His teeth were black and his eyes red and bloodshot. He looked to be about seventeen years old, but later I found out that he was barely thirteen. I moved nearer to him but dared not say anything. I supposed he was crazy and feared he might embarrass me publicly. I wanted to walk away, but suddenly I wondered whether this is how Jesus would have behaved. Ashamed of my feelings, I approached the boy, told him my name, and asked him if he would allow me to teach him how to become a mechanic. He told me that his name was Agaba and asked if there was anything else I could teach. I replied that I could teach him to repair televisions and radios, and added that I would be paying him for taking these courses. I had realized that some sort of incentive was necessary to enable me to reach these children who were so far removed from normality. I invited him to come to the Rohana Club on Thursday at two o'clock in the afternoon if he was interested. Before noon, I had talked to and invited over thirty boys.

The Rohana Club had once been an Asian social club, but Amin's soldiers had taken it over as a boxing club. Before the Liberation War was over, it had practically turned into a human slaughterhouse. The fleeing soldiers had left the place in total disarray. Combat uniforms, boots, and magazines littered the floor, which in places was covered with bloodstains. And now the Custodian Board of the new government had allocated the property to Africa Foundation to provide the first children's home in Kampala. Semakula, our first houseparent, worked tirelessly cleaning and scrubbing to prepare the building for habitation. Nakafero and her children were the first to move in, and they helped to complete the job.

On the following Thursday in June of 1979, I walked to the club and found some of the children I had invited gathered in one room. I was pleased to see the tar boy, Agaba. First I assured the children that we were going to form a home. We would be a family, and I would see to it that they were provided for. Then I explained my plan for teaching them the skills I had promised. Before the meeting ended, the children asked if they could appoint a leader to be responsible for their behavior and discipline. Steve Tumuhairiwe was elected captain. Steve actually held an East African certificate of education, but like many others, he had abandoned formal education for the easy money of the black market. So the first Africa Foundation home was opened in Kampala on June 29, 1979, a day that would be celebrated in the following years. On the first anniversary, Steve made a speech telling the story of the first days of our home.

"My friends, at first it was a tug-of-war to convince the children who were known as *bayaye* to come to this home. Because of Amin's regime, we were suspicious of anyone who came to talk to us. Previously many of us had been put in prison for such crimes as cutting down sugar cane or other acts done only to try to keep ourselves alive, so we considered everyone an enemy. Despite these challenges, Reverend Sempangi did not get discouraged. He tried to convince us to trust him and persuaded us in many different ways to come to the home. Within a week, he had collected forty children.

"The first weeks after the opening were difficult. We had nothing in the home. We slept on the bare concrete floor, but there we found something we had not found anywhere else. In the home we found love. We did not get discouraged. After all, we had shelter, where before we had been sleeping in the gutters. In November of that first year, the Uganda Blanket Manufacturing Company donated fifty blankets to our home. In December, the Embassy of Iraq gave us fourteen bunk beds. In January of the next year, Sarah Cox and other Americans came with cups, blankets, bedsheets, towels, and a Land Rover. Unfortunately the Land Rover was stolen in May.

"On the 28th of January 1980, we had a historic day in this home. The first group of *bayaye* went to school. We held a party in honor of these thirty-eight children. We had become *bayaye*, not because we liked the life, but because we were forced to by our circumstances. We smoked *bhangi* and blew our brains with petroleum fumes because this was our only blanket against the cold. Thanks to this home and the efforts of Reverend Sempangi, we were rescued from that life. This will be a story to be told in the future."

A VOICE IN THE DARKNESS

What a blessing it was to see lives transformed in such a way, but there had been a time in the beginning days of the home that I was almost persuaded to quit and leave Uganda altogether. My doubts began one Friday before the minister of supplies was appointed. Sarah Cox, the American from Mississippi who had insisted on coming to Uganda, came to talk with me. As she approached, she saw a crowd of people pushing each other to enter my office. They were fighting to get little chits, or ration coupons, from me to be used to obtain essential commodities like sugar, soap, soda, and salt. Even if a person found someone selling these items, he was forced to go to one of the ministers to obtain a chit before he was allowed to purchase it.

People were desperate to get the chits, and the distribution points were maddening. It was somewhat a survival of the fittest to navigate the crowds of eager people to get even one. To many, it was a matter of life and death. Sometimes people who fought their way through the mob and received a chit would go outside and sell it at an exorbitant price. A genuine seeker had no choice but to pay and to regard himself as lucky to have gotten it at any price.

Sarah Cox sat in my office patiently waiting for a chance to talk to me. She was sure that eventually I would tire or lose my temper and have to take a break. Finally I squeezed in a few minutes to listen to her.

Her first statement to me was shocking. "Kefa, are you a government minister or an office manager?" I was so taken aback that I could not answer. She continued, "If you are a minister, why are you spending so much time and effort on such a menial task as handing out chits?" Then her voice changed and was filled with compassion. "Kefa, why are you so determined to stay in Uganda? You know you are not safe. There are still those who would like to see a man of God like you dead." Then she handed me an airline ticket. "Please take this ticket and leave Uganda. You can return when it is safe. Many other returnees have already had to flee for their lives. It will be no shame for you to go now."

Her words gave me much to consider, and I spent much time agonizing over what I should do. Yes, Uganda was a dangerous place, with the necessity for curfews every other day and with shootings every night. The police patrolled the streets and arrests were made at every turn. On the other hand, we had just opened a home for street children, and the youngsters were depending on me for food, clothing, protection, and even their education. I had also begun a Presbyterian church, the first one of its kind in Uganda. If I left, what would I be saying to the new believers? Was my God not sufficient for times like these? If I left the work, surely it would crumble. And then there were my duties in the government. So many people were depending upon me. But was Sarah correct? Was my life really in danger to the extent that I needed to run? Not only did I have pressure from friends, but also there were questions from within that were tearing me apart.

On Sunday I preached a sermon about Moses's call. God had wanted to send Moses to deliver his people from Egypt. In their encounter when Moses had expressed doubt and insecurity, God asked Moses, "What is in your hand?" to which Moses replied, "A stick." Suddenly I realized that this brief exchange was in itself a challenge to me and my people. Just as God was calling Moses to do a monumental task when all he had at hand was a stick, so God was calling us to a great work, knowing full well our limited resources. We had not yet caught the vision of what great things God would do with our meager contributions. Perhaps he would use a small talent, our weaknesses, or even a stick to accomplish our complete deliverance. I was rebuked by the words of Zechariah 4:10: "Despise not the day of small things."

I did not immediately realize the impact of that sermon upon my own life. As a matter of fact, I drove back to my hotel somehow perturbed by my own sermon.

At suppertime I happened to sit at the table with a famous poet and university lecturer, Peter Btek. He started a debate on the poor spirituality of the West versus the rich spirituality of the Jewish religion. Normally the topic would have intrigued me, but I had my own deep confusion and chose not to participate in the discussion.

I returned to my room and decided to take a shower. I had just lathered up completely when suddenly the water ran out. Frustrated, I took the soap and towel in my hand and stepped out of the shower. As I did, what should happen but the power went off, leaving me in utter darkness. I could not see even one inch ahead of me and felt what it would be like to be totally blind. I had to walk with my hand up to avoid hitting anything. Of course, everything was motionless. There was not a single sound of anything, not even the whistle from the tap. "Is it time to pray?" I thought to myself. No, I had learned never to go before God when I am in a fighting or quarreling mood, for Scripture tells us to "enter His gates with thanksgiving" (Ps 100:4). I also thought of Ecclesiastes 5:2, which admonishes us, "Be not rash with thy mouth and let not thine heart be hasty to utter anything before God."

I stood in my room speechless, but in the middle of this despair there came a revelation, so clear and reassuring. "Kefa, take this soap and this towel and wash the children of Uganda." What a relief it was to know with assurance just exactly what God's will was for me! God spoke to my heart so distinctly that it was as clear as if he had spoken to my ears. The doubt, fear, and confusion fled, and peace flooded my heart.

My life changed forever that day. My path had been clearly directed by my loving and all-wise Father. I gave myself one hundred percent to the direct calling of God and determined not to quit or turn back. When I look back upon my life and consider the many experiences that I have encountered, I have to say that the most influential moment was that marvelous day when God showed me the way.

Within a few weeks I was there at the Rohana Club with Nakafero, washing the children of Uganda and scrubbing their teeth, which had not seen a toothbrush for years. It was like cleaning soot from a once painted wall.

Unfortunately, Sarah Cox and George Hansburg were the ones who had to flee Uganda. One night in August of 1979, soldiers were making a routine patrol of Bakuli where Sarah and George were renting the house of Mulira, but the dogs that Mulira had left behind refused to allow anyone into the enclosure around the house. Irritated by the violent barking of the dogs, the soldiers began shooting bullets into the air, rocking the place and frightening the entire neighborhood. Bullets were even shot through the top of the corrugated roof, causing a deafening noise. Sarah and George felt sure that they were the targets. Nothing would stop the dogs from barking, and the barrage continued for three long, agonizing hours.

Very early the next morning, Situka hurried to the hotel to report this incident to me. I drove to the site and was startled by the number of bullet shells that were scattered around the compound. It was as if thousands of grasshoppers had invaded. By the time I arrived, George and his family and Sarah had already packed their personal belongings and were ready to leave. They took a bus to Nairobi the same day. How ironic and sad that it was actually Sarah who was in more danger than I!

AYUB

A scarcity of supplies for the children was not the only difficulty we faced. The children who came to us were encumbered with severe problems. Although our ultimate goal was to lead these precious souls to Jesus Christ, we found it necessary to first present a sense of humanity to them and to teach them what love was. When they were able to become more than animals, then they would be able to comprehend the love of God and respond to it. Ayub was an example of such a need.

Ayub was among the first group of eleven children to join the home. Among the others were Nakafero's three children, Topista, Namusisi, and Nora. I learned a great deal from these children. Ayub was a nine-year-old boy with the experiences of an adult. He even talked like an adult. He had spent four years sleeping in the latrine near the Nakivubo Stadium. His family had lived in the suburbs of Kampala near the prison in Luzira. His father had been a peasant farmer but had died after a brief illness. His mother cooked outside in the open or in rainy weather on the veranda.

During the Liberation War, Amin's soldiers had camped near their house. One evening before dark, one of the soldiers told Ayub's mother to surrender all her food. The woman declared that the food was for herself and her son. The angry soldiers kicked the food from her hands and hit her in the head. Small Ayub started to run. He kept on running and planned to run out of Uganda. He ran as far as he could go, and convinced that he was out of the country, he entered an unfinished building. He thought it was a ditch in which to hide. The next morning, Ayub found himself numb and partially paralyzed. He managed to get to Kampala and saw people going in and coming out of a public toilet. He entered and locked himself in this toilet and refused to allow anyone to disturb him. This was his new home.

He always entered the toilet after eleven at night and was careful to wake up before six in the morning. During the days he collected cellophane paper from the garbage heaps and sold it in the market. He noticed that even the street children did not like to go near him, and he realized that they were repelled by his disgusting smell. Many times Ayub wished he were dead. The day I met him, he had taken excessive *bhangi* and petroleum fumes, and was close to death. I was able to rescue him by taking him to the home and giving him the love he so desperately needed and deserved.

Ayub later told me that the home had made him human. One morning as I was chatting with him at Rohana, I saw a notorious boy fighting my best-loved girl, Namusisi. These fights were very common in the home. Ayub told me that these fights were helping the children to build strong relationships, but I could not tolerate the way Monday hit Namusisi. After I stopped the fight and dried Namusisi's tears, Ayub made an amazing revelation. He said, "Daddy, you have seen us fighting or being beaten by the mob, but you have never seen a tear in our eyes." I realized that now Namusisi was able to cry because she knew that I loved her and cared for her. These children had forgotten how to be children, and now it was coming back to them. Namusisi's tears were a result of her newly found humanity.

A lady evangelist visited the children's home and found Ayub on the veranda. She asked him, "Have you ever been converted from your sins?"

"Why don't you ask me whether I have ever been converted from my poverty?" he replied.

Annoyed at his response, she marched straight to my office to express disgust. She was concerned that I was teaching the children a social gospel. I took the opportunity to show the lady how even the Lord used human needs as a pre-evangelism strategy. I used the story of the man at the pool of Bethesda as an example.

Evidently she did not understand my point and replied, "What these children need is the gospel."

"Well, if you can see that these children need the gospel, what is stopping you from also seeing that they need clean water, adequate food, a good shelter, and medical attention?" I continued to explain that when Jesus spoke of the kingdom of God, he meant a society on earth in which God's will is done as it is in heaven. This society cannot become a reality to a people in bondage. God never gave the Ten Commandments to his people while they were in Egypt. The law was given after the people were taken from the house of bondage. I wanted the lady evangelist to understand that the love we give to the children by relieving them from their bondage of poverty will open the door to their understanding of God's love and make them ready to receive him. In their poverty they were not able to understand the concept of love at all. I pointed her to Psalm 82, where God is very clear that if his people neglect their duty to the poor and the fatherless, then the whole world is off course. The downtrodden need to be delivered from their darkness of repression before they can be delivered from their darkness of sin.

I do not think that what I said ever met the expectations of the lady evangelist.

> Defend the poor and fatherless: do justice to the afflicted and needy. Deliver the poor and needy: rid them out of the hand of the wicked. (Ps 82:3–4)

5

Nakafero's Death and Legacy

INITIALLY THE WORK OF Africa Foundation was rehabilitation. Our goal was to restore normalcy by providing for material needs and by establishing moral conditions for children whose past and future had been shattered. Many of these children had witnessed their parents' brutal murders right before their very eyes. How difficult was our task in a country in which one step forward seemed to be followed by two steps backward! The legacy of moral bankruptcy had had far-reaching implications by impacting every nook and cranny of our society.

Nakafero and her children possessed nothing, but they lived together as a family, occupying one small room at the newly acquired home at Rohana Club. The poor living conditions and the daily worries of life had taken their toll on Nakafero. She suffered from high blood pressure, and her legs were swollen. Nakafero consistently refused to go to the hospital because she had her own fears about modern medicine. She maintained that the medicine used by doctors was dangerous. Actually, medicine was rare in the country. Some relief drugs had arrived soon after the liberation, but these were either sold on the black market or smuggled out of the country. Nakafero had seen people in the market filling capsules with corn flour and selling them as medicine. She told me that it had become common practice to bribe a doctor before one could receive any medicine. She was surprised that I wanted to send her for an operation to a hospital where even people of position had died on the operating table for lack of oxygen. If many important people could die in the hospitals, what chance would a beggar woman like herself have? Mulago, a five-hundred-bed hospital and the largest in the country, had no running water and had a serious shortage of oxygen. I sympathized with Nakafero's fears. She told me that her medicine was my return to Uganda, because she knew I would take care of her children after her death.

In the first week of September of 1979, I received an emergency telephone call from the houseparent of the children's home, Fred Semakula, notifying me that Nakafero was dying. The call came about three thirty in the morning, and in those days it was suicide to go out after eight in the evening or before dawn. I put down the receiver, but I could not go back to sleep. I thought of many things I should have done for this woman to make her happy. In the morning I hired a taxi to go to see her. When I got to the home, I saw what I had expected—Nakafero surrounded by the children. I told the children to leave the room and began to hum "The Song of Simeon." Finally, with a weak whisper, Nakafero spoke. "This time I am going, but God is merciful. He has kept me until you returned. I have no relatives, so you decide where to bury me."

Topista, her daughter, had come back into the room, and I told her to join me in "The Song of Simeon." But before the song was over, I was on my feet saying, "Nakafero, Simeon asked God to let him depart because his eyes had seen the Salvation of God." I continued boldly, "You are dying, but what have you seen? Why should you die while you are still eating crumbs? You should live to see God's redemption of this land!" I spoke to her as if she had some control over her death. She was in agony; her legs were bloated and soft, swollen with fluid. The last suggestions I would have ever offered her were to go to the hospital or even to call a doctor. My only option was to pray for her recovery.

Miraculously, Nakafero improved. Realizing that one of the causes of her ill health was her poor diet, I organized some food supplements. The change of diet greatly improved her health. Even her complexion cleared, but her legs remained swollen.

At the beginning of 1980, Nakafero came to me with a suggestion to buy a piece of land where she could settle. She felt that the home, which was established for children, was not the right place for her to live. Nakafero had not been idle in recruiting children for the home. She and her children had brought more than fifty children from the markets of Owino and Shauri Yako to live and recover at the Rohana Club. But she felt it was time to leave.

Nakafero found a suitable piece of land at Kirinya, about fourteen miles away on Kampala-Hoima Road. Africa Foundation paid for the land, and she took her own children and moved to the new premises where they all engaged in farming. At the same time, the children attended a neighboring Christian school. They grew bananas, maize, cassava, and sweet potatoes and even sold much of her produce to the foundation. Our dear Nakafero, for the first time in her life, had become a producer rather than a beggar. This change in her life tremendously improved her opinion of herself and further strengthened her faith in God. Her life was living evidence of genuine rehabilitation.

Nakafero had a happy and fulfilling life with her girls for several years, but in the spring of 1982, the tide turned for her family. Very early one morning, I heard Namusisi and Nora at the door knocking and crying loudly. I recognized the voices clearly, but what were they saying? Could I possibly be hearing correctly? The words pierced my heart when I realized the cry was "Come quickly; our mother has been shot dead!" When I got to the door, I was met by the sobbing girls and saw Topista running to join them, choked with sorrow and pointing at her neck and stomach to signify the areas where her mother had been shot.

I accompanied the grieving girls back to their home and found Nakafero's body lying outside her house in the now-deserted village. Topista explained that on Sunday evening, ten bandits had come to the house with clubs and guns. One of the thugs, a resident of the same village, had pointed at Nakafero. She had begged her killers to allow her to pray, but as she prayed, they shot her in the neck and stomach. The girls stood by, frozen with fear. As the bandits were leaving, one bandit shook hands with the gunmen and complimented them on a job well done. The frightened children gathered around their dead mother, but hearing more shots, they were forced to desert the body and flee into the bush, where they spent the night in sorrow and fear. While in the bush, Topista remembered the words the preacher had read that very morning from Psalm 37, "Fret not thyself because of evil doers neither be thou envious against the workers of iniquity: For they shall soon be cut down like the grass and wither as the green herb" (vv. 1–2). God's Word comforted her through the night.

Nakafero's burial on her own plot of land was attended by many of the children from the home. Earlier she had insisted that she not be given traditional African funeral rites, but be buried by the Book, so that is just what we did. After the funeral, I visited with a distant relative of Nakafero. He informed me that she had told him that if anything happened to her, it was her unwritten will that her children were to be placed in the care of Kefa (myself).

The work of Africa Foundation brought disappointments and challenges. We learned that we would always be frustrated if we expected to see instant results in the lives of those to whom we ministered. Rehabilitation was a long and slow process that required transformations in the social and moral fabric of society. We saw successes and failures, and experienced joys and sadness. But when we were able to reach out to a precious soul, to give him the love for which he was starving, and to point him to the heavenly Father, who loved him with the greatest of all love, we received great satisfaction. Although we were grieved to lose Nakafero, we were comforted by the fact that she was with her Father and would be rejoicing evermore. How thrilling it was to know that the love of God working through us had made all the difference in her life and in the lives of her children!

Of all the Africans I have ever known, Nakafero was the one who made the most powerful impact upon my life. I always considered her to have been the real founder of Africa Foundation, for she had been my inspiration. She had been like a mother to me, encouraging me, challenging me, and even correcting me at times. I loved her and will always miss her. The children at Rohana loved her too. As poor in earthly possessions as she was, she left behind a tremendous legacy. She was rich in wisdom, rich in compassion, and rich in love.

> Her children arise up, and call her blessed . . . Many daughters have done virtuously, but thou excellest them all. (Prov 31:28–29)

6

Namusisi

S HE WAS DIRTY AND dusty. Her curly hair had seen neither a comb nor
water for months. In one hand she carried a package of cigarettes and
in the other a solvent rag. I approached her under the pretense of buying
a cigarette from her, and then to get closer to her, I asked her to help me
light it. During the exchange she realized that I had no interest in smoking
and called my bluff. I quickly introduced myself and told her that, rather
than cigarettes, I was actually interested in her. She told me her name was
Namusisi, but since it was nearly curfew, she did not have time to talk to
me. I left her a little money and promised to meet her the following day
at the same time and place. I had hardly moved two meters when I saw
a gang of boys almost tearing her to pieces. The boys wanted to take the
money from her, but she refused to let them. This girl had the stamina for
self-defense and was well able to fight back and protect herself.

Street children are frightening to the general public. They themselves
are extremely vulnerable to the hazards of living on the street. They are
susceptible to disease, rape, violence, and drug abuse. As I drove away,
I could tell that Namusisi was suffering from a sense of self-rejection.
Internally she was bleeding from deep psychological wounds that had re-
sulted in a negative self-image. As a street child, she was forced to resort
to violence in order to adapt to the hostile environment into which she
had been thrust. I could not help pitying her as I returned to the hotel.

The following day I went back just as I had promised. I was careful
to keep appointments that I made with street children in order to earn
their trust and to establish strong relationships with them. I left the car
with my two Tanzanian escorts around a corner so as not to intimidate
the children. Also I wore jeans and a gray T-shirt so that perhaps I would
better blend into the culture of the street urchins. As I walked down the
noisy street, I remembered the words of the Apostle Paul: "And unto the

Jews I became as a Jew, that I might gain the Jews . . . To the weak became I as weak, that I might gain the weak: I am made all things to all men, that I might by all means save some" (1 Cor 9:20a, 22).

Namusisi was waiting for me at the same place we had met the day before. She was wearing the same linen and apparently had not washed her face. As I approached her, I asked, "Namusisi, where is my cigarette?"

She replied laughing, "I know you don't smoke!"

The same boys I had seen the day before were watching. In fact, I heard one calling in a teasing manner, "There comes Namusisi's boyfriend."

When I mentioned the fight with the boys, she replied confidently, "I have my money. They can't manage me!"

I told Namusisi about the Rohana Club and about the opportunities I could offer her there. It did not take bribes or convincing for her to agree to go with me. She eagerly jumped into the car and was ready to go. I then invited the five boys who were watching us, and they too gladly climbed into the car. Sadly these boys had been sniffing solvent, chewing *kirt* (a stimulant), and smoking marijuana. As we drove away, I looked in the rear view mirror and saw three other boys running after us. I stopped and let them join the group. When we reached Rohana, we had nine recruits with us. I left Nakafero, who was still living at the time, and Fred Semakula preparing rooms for them. Soon Namusisi was able to start school at Mengo.

I wondered how such a lovely girl as this had ended up on the streets in such a miserable life, so one day I asked her to tell me her story.

"My parents," she explained, "were residents of Rubaga, a section of Kampala. My father was killed by one of Amin's soldiers. I returned home one evening to find his body lying on the floor in a pool of blood, his face battered beyond recognition. I was horrified and burst into wailing, but my mother quickly silenced me. She whispered to me that the soldier who had murdered my father was still in the bedroom.

"After a while, the soldier left the house, and my mother turned to me and told me that I could then start crying. Some neighbors joined me in my mourning, and the following day we buried my father. Right after the burial, my mother took me with her to join the murderous soldier at Naguru Barracks. She was going to become his new wife!

"I was filled with resentment and hatred against this horrible man. Every time I looked at him, I remembered my father's battered head lying in the cold pool of blood. I was also angry with my mother. I saw her as a traitor to my father and a deserter. How could she care for this man who was so evil and had brought so much torment to our family?

"One evening, this soldier came home drunk. Standing at the threshold, he ordered me to get out of the house. It was dark and I had nowhere to go, but as I left the barracks, I was neither sad nor lonely. It was such a relief to be away from the haunting figure of this wicked man.

"That night I slept at the bus park, and the place became my home. I quickly learned the ways of the street in order to survive the harassments of life. It was there that Daddy found me and brought me to a new and happy life."

In 1980, a relative of Namusisi brought sad news to my office. Namusisi's mother had died. I sent for the girl, who was at school, to give her the awful news. I agonized within myself as to how I could possibly break the news to her. When she arrived, I took her aside to tell her in private. At first she hesitated, and then she burst into laughter. When she saw my shocked expression, she quickly explained, "My mother died a long time ago when she ran away with the soldier."

Namusisi refused to attend her mother's burial. Instead she went to her room and composed a song that later became the Africa Foundation children's anthem.

AFRICA FOUNDATION ANTHEM

We had no hope in this world
That we would ever be people.
He helped, guided, and made us his children.
We pray, Daddy, that you live long.

Chorus:
Africa Foundation is our group.
It is led by Dr. Kefa Sempangi.
It has helped us children of God.
We pray, Daddy, that you live long.

We did not have clothes and food;
We did not have school fees for school.
Yet without school these days, no way to go,
Now we are in school. Thank you, Daddy. You saved us.

Namusisi

We are advising you, children of Africa Foundation,
To work hard with pens and books.
We will rejoice when we all overcome
And remember that Daddy saved us.

Daddy Kefa, we congratulate you,
For the power and strength you have shown us.
We pray that you live long.
We shall help you when you are old.

7

The Dust House

W HEN I LEFT AMERICA to attend the Moshi conference in the spring of 1979, I had to leave my wife and children in the United States. And then when I left Moshi to return to Uganda as a member of the new government, they were still unable to join me because of the continued unrest in the country. It was not until September of that year that it was possible for them to join me in Uganda. We were so happy to finally be together again. For three months we stayed in the Nile Mansions, a local hotel, because the house we were planning to live in at Bakuli, which was only a mile from Rohana Club, was under repair. The children in the home were eager for us to come and live near them. They wanted my company no matter what ugly conditions I lived in. I was the one who had first earned their trust, and I was the one totally responsible for them. I was the one who loved them, and they knew that. They were beginning to love me back.

Late one evening, I was visited by other thoughts. Maybe I should take the house at Summit View in Kololo. It was a lovely place to live, and my family would be so happy there. I remembered the words of my friend John Perkins: "In reaching the poor, we must never antagonize the rich." Would associating more with the wealthier people be beneficial to our work? I was aware that I needed to be a viable bridge between the rich and the poor in order to allow the goods to cross. What would be wrong with providing a lovely home for my wife and children?

I suddenly realized that I was allowing materialism to sidetrack me from my work. I had transferred my resources to the children, and now I needed to relocate myself. I wanted to be one-hundred-percent committed to the task that God had so clearly assigned. I decided firmly to move to Bakuli. However, even after I had made the decision to join the children, Satan did not give up on his efforts to tempt me to a finer life.

A week before our move, two social workers came to see me. They tried desperately to convince me not to live in the house at Bakuli, as it was not a house befitting a man of my status. A government minister, they argued, needed to make a strong statement to the people with his position of affluence.

Nevertheless, in a few days we made the move to Plot No. 7, Hoima Road, Bakuli. Immediately my children gave the house its nickname. They called it "the dust house." Dust of several decades had accumulated on the roofs of many of the surrounding buildings as well as on our own roof. Dust seemed to be everywhere and on everything. The area had been populated by Indians and other Asians, and reflected their culture. The inhabitants had been forced to abandon their settlement when Amin had forced all Asians into exile.

In one of our evening devotions, I shared with my family about the time Jesus fed the five thousand with only five loaves of bread and two fish. At the end of the meal, Jesus ordered his disciples to collect the leftovers. There were twelve baskets, one for each disciple. Dawudi, my young son, wanted to know when our basket was to come. Damali had already observed that the houses of parliamentarians were better homes than ours. We had sold our house in America, and there was no comparison between that middle-class home and the Bakuli house into which we moved. They saw our new house as a demotion. I saw that I needed to pray that my children would understand my vision for the street children and would be willing to sacrifice along with me in order to provide a better life for others. I certainly did not want them to be consumed by the materialism that they had seen abroad.

There were many positive aspects to our new home, however. It was an old sprawling Asian-style building with five living rooms, two sitting rooms, and two large corridors. Moving from room to room was quite easy, but the openness of the house left us little privacy. We had room for many of the former street children to live with us. Sometimes the new ones would stay with us until there was room for them in the home. The notorious big boys would stay with us, along with children who had become unmanageable for the houseparents. The best aspect of our house was that it was accessible to all. It was an open house to the children, to the neighbors, and to our relatives. Sometimes it appeared more like a social center or a hospital than a private home.

My living with the children broke down many barriers. Being in contact with them day in and day out led me to a greater understanding of their problems and their needs. Getting them to the home was simply the beginning of a very long process. We had to allow time for social adjustment. They had to learn that there were social norms and values in civilized society. They had to learn to trust and to love.

One little girl explained the problem very clearly to me one night after supper, and unknowingly gave me my first lesson in understanding the children.

"Daddy," she said, "I think there is a big difference between eating food and having a meal. I never had the opportunity in my life where I sat down and ate food with other people. In the market and on the street, we are always on the run. Maybe, Daddy, that could be the reason that when you make us sit at the table to eat our food, we fight because we are not used to this kind of life. But, Daddy, don't worry. We are learning. You will soon be happy with us."

Fred Semakula, who had been our first houseparent at Kasubi in 1971, was now the first houseparent at Rohana in 1979. He, too, was very happy to see me staying with the children at Bakuli. One afternoon he brought about ten children fresh from the Natete Market. The youngest was about six and the oldest not more than nine. They arrived about four o'clock in the afternoon, and we began our same routine of cleaning them. Dinner was late that evening, so I decided to serve them tea while we waited. I got them started and left to take a shower. When I returned, what a sight I found! They were tearing at each other, fighting with the bitterest form of animosity, and using the cups as stones to hit each other. Five cups were lying broken in hundreds of pieces on the floor. They had torn the handles off the plastic cups, and the teapot was in the corner with a child squatting on it.

Although inwardly I suddenly felt overwhelmed by the task before me, outwardly I remained surprisingly calm. Since the little girl had explained the fighting to me, I was prepared to deal with it in an understanding manner. I gathered the children around me in a nearby sitting room and read a Bible story to them. They listened attentively, and then I taught them to sing "Jesus Loves Me, This I know, For the Bible tells me so." They seemed to enjoy the singing, though I am sure they did not comprehend the scope of the simple song. Nevertheless, it was a start. They had seen me deal patiently with their poor habits and had felt a touch of gentle love. One day they would know the love of their heavenly Father, which surpasses all love. It would just take time and patience.

By the time the children had learned the song, dinner was ready. We went back to the same table, but this time there was no fighting because I was careful not to leave the room (another lesson learned!). However, I noticed that they were secretly pinching one another under the table, thinking that I would not see them. I said nothing, as I realized that this was just their way of getting to know each other.

After supper, we had time to pray together. By the end of the prayer time, Nanfuka, the housekeeper, had spread mattresses on the floor and made the beds, such as they were. It did not take long for all the children to fall asleep.

Around two o'clock in the morning, I was awakened by strange noises coming from the children's room. "Oh no," I thought to myself, "the children are fighting again." I considered getting a stick to go and discipline them, but off hand I did not know where a stick was. Certainly I had no stick in the house. I walked slowly down the corridor to see what was going on, and peeked cautiously around the corner, lest some object come flying at me and hit me in the head. I was shocked when I saw the children all asleep on their mattresses. Although they were asleep, they were tossing and crying aloud. I realized that they were having nightmares, and some were hallucinating. What a pitiful sight they were! I did not wake them but returned to my bed and went back to sleep.

A short time later some American ladies who had come to Uganda to help with the work of Africa Foundation came to Bakuli. I told the ladies about the nasty experiences I had with the children at night. One lady who had studied medicine and psychology at the University of California was extremely helpful in her explanation of their behavior. She told me that she had seen the same thing in Latin American children who were suffering the same type of trauma. She explained that some of these children had come from good stable homes where they were loved and properly cared for. Their families had been subjected to Amin's treacherous regime, their parents had been killed, and the children were disbanded and traumatized. The children were completely denied the necessary parental touch and care.

Now with a mattress, a blanket, a pillow, and a good meal, their hearts heard echoes of their lost comfort and security. We would hear children crying in their sleep, "Mama!" because the new comforts brought back images of their mothers and their homes. She encouraged us that as they began to feel safe and loved, they would adjust and have fewer and fewer nightmares.

The lady was also able to give us several other helpful tips. First, she admonished us not to give the new arrivals warm food. Many of the street children had been eating cold garbage from the dumps for a long time. Their intestinal linings and enzymes had adjusted to the cold, unhygienic food. A sudden, drastic change in diet could cause serious abdominal pain. She advised us to give the children things like pawpaws, pineapples, and sweet bananas for a few days, and then graduate from there to warm food.

She also noticed that many of the children were coughing badly, and when she examined their skin, she found ringworm. We realized that the children desperately needed treatment for worms. Amazingly after the treatment, the coughing disappeared. This fact was a wonderful revelation to me because I had never associated coughing with worms in the stomach. We began treating the children for worms every two months, and the incidence of disease was greatly reduced.

With so many children together, it would have been easy to incorporate policies and methods that would, in the long run, have dehumanized them. I had to be careful to keep a home environment rather than that of an institution. A professor of sociology at Makerere University in Kampala sent some of his students to study the behavior of the street children in a home environment. I refused to give them access to the children because such a study would have reduced our children to the level of guinea pigs.

At the beginning of our work, the city council assigned five social workers to join me in the new endeavor of rehabilitating the young displaced boys and girls. I asked the social workers to write the history and background of each child, but they surprised me by referring to each one as a client or as case number such and such. I know that social workers are trained to keep a distance from their clients, but the therapy that these children needed was our personal involvement. I instructed the workers always to use names to refer to the children.

It is interesting that the Bible points out instances of Christ's healing multitudes of sick people in one verse, but the same Bible will spend almost a whole chapter telling about the healing of one individual. God cares about groups, but groups are made up of individuals, and each one is important to him. In Isaiah 43:1, we are told that God knows us by name. Certainly we are not clients or case numbers to him. I was determined to do everything possible to reflect God's love and compassion to each child in my care.

The professor of sociology from Makerere University came to Rohana and advised one of the social workers to write some regulations and to hang them on the wall. The rules stated such dictations as when the children were to get up in the morning, when they were to do their chores, and when they were to go to bed. One afternoon, I found these detailed regulations posted on the wall, and I became furious. I called the social worker to my office and told her to her face that I had established a children's home, and I had no desire to make it into an institution. Moreover, I reminded the lady that she herself was a mother of five children, and I asked her whether she had regulations posted on the walls of her home. I think she understood my position, as we saw no more regulations on the walls.

One day the professor came to my office for a serious encounter. He wanted to know in which institute I had studied sociology. My blood began to boil, and I am afraid that I did not have a very positive response to him. I told him that I had seen many large families, and I wondered what institute of sociology the parents of those families had attended to become mothers and fathers. I asked the professor to kindly allow me to become a father of many children.

Later on, the professor and I became friends, and he would send many of his students to do their internships with us. He explained to them that they would be learning "an alternative approach to sociology." A working relationship had been established between Africa Foundation and Makerere University, where I subsequently was invited to serve on the panel of external examiners in the school of fine art and design.

8

Habitat for Humanity

HAVING RETURNED TO MY country as a member of the National Consultative Council, which was actually an interim government, I was soon appointed deputy minister in the Department of Rehabilitation. My job was to assist the widows and orphans whose heads of family had been killed between 1971 and 1979. The number of widows who had registered by then was more than 300,000. These were women with traumatic memories, and many had severe psychological damage. Some had experienced acts far too inhuman and obscene to describe.

In my capacity as deputy minister of rehabilitation, I was taken around the various sites where Amin's henchmen had dumped the bodies of their victims. I was taken first to the State Research Bureau at Nakasero, and then representatives of the bureau drove me to Namanve Forest, which is nine miles east of Kampala on the Kampala-Jinja Highway. As we drove through the forest, my guides pulled up to a spot they wanted me to see. They stopped the vehicle, and we walked a short way through the woods. They pointed out the very spot where Dora Bloch, an elderly Jewish woman, had been burned to death during the raid on Entebbe. Her gray hair did not catch fire, so the people could tell that it was a white person's body. We walked farther, and I was aghast to see the remains of many human bodies left in the forest to decay. Occasionally the rotting rags of the victims rustled and fluttered in the gentle breeze. As I looked at the carcasses, I realized that these silent, deteriorating bones had been the fathers of the precious children who were now roaming the streets of the cities, the husbands of the emotionally damaged wives who were now left destitute. I understood why the widows could not answer their children's questions: "Where is my father?" and "If my father is dead, where is he buried?" Amin had been so callused and demonic that he had never even considered putting his victims in a grave of any kind. He dumped them in forests, burned them, and even fed them to the crocodiles.

Quite often I spent hours wondering if God had any concern for the suffering humanity in Uganda. I asked the old question, how could He have let this happen? I understood Isaiah's mourning over the desolation of Jerusalem. "Thy holy cities are a wilderness, Zion is a wilderness, Jerusalem a desolation. Our holy and our beautiful house, where our fathers praised thee, is burned up with fire: and all our pleasant things are laid waste. Wilt thou refrain thyself for these things, O LORD? Wilt thou hold thy peace, and afflict us very sore?" (Isa 64:10–12).

But eventually God's loving Spirit brought Scripture to my mind to console me. Ezra had also faced the destruction of Jerusalem and was given the task of rebuilding the temple. As he confessed the sins of his people, he also recognized the grace and mercy that God was extending to his generation. Rather than to wallow in the misery of the past, he was grateful for the new opportunities that lay before him: "And now for a little space grace hath been shewed from the LORD our God, to leave us a remnant to escape, and to give us a nail in his holy place, that our God may lighten our eyes, and give us a little reviving in our bondage. For we were bondmen; yet our God hath not forsaken us in our bondage, but hath extended mercy unto us" (Ezra 9:8–9a). Yes, terrible things had happened because of the evil in the world. Satan is a powerful force of evil who stirs up pain and grief wherever he can. But God does not leave us alone in our grief. Just as he offered his Son as a relief from our bondage in sin, so he is there with us to give us relief from our bondage of physical suffering and poverty.

Although God did not cause the terrible suffering of the people of Uganda, he was now using the destruction of the country as an open door for the Africa Foundation to bring healing and salvation to the hungry souls. As we ministered to their physical needs, the hearts of the people would be opened to hear the cure for their spiritual needs. Through death and destruction, Life would be brought to Uganda.

With so many problems in Uganda, it was difficult to know where to start. In 1970, Uganda had reached one of the highest per-capita incomes in East Africa, but during the reign of Idi Amin, we experienced a rapid economic decline. It is estimated that between 1971 and 1979 both exports and imports fell by sixty percent. With drastic drops in domestic production, the scarcity of imports, and uncontrolled monetary expansion, we experienced rampant inflation. In 1980, eighty-five percent of the children under the age of six had never had the privilege of sleeping under a blanket. From Amin's evil leadership and from the economic collapse of the country emanated massive corruption, smuggling, bribery, looting, and genocide. We needed recovery in every area—political, moral, economic, and spiritual.

One of the worst poverty-stricken areas was Gulu in northern Uganda. Out of a population of 270,185, there were an estimated 10,000 widows. This meant that for every twenty-seven people, there was a widow. Because of Amin's atrocities, these women were struggling desperately to survive with no one to help them or their children. In 1979, I took a trip to Gulu to see what could be done to provide the assistance they needed.

When I arrived, Bishop Kihangire took me on a tour of the area in his car. This car, like most cars in Uganda, was not much more than a dilapidated jalopy. It was impossible to obtain spare auto parts, so when something went bad, the owners were forced to make the best of it. Our engine kept overheating, so we were compelled to make frequent stops to let it cool. As we traveled and stopped for engine cooling, I noticed that there was one item that seemed to be prolific in the area. Mango trees were everywhere, and they were loaded with mangoes. Every tree had a crowd of people under it, cooling in the shade and eating the mangoes. We saw people walking down the road eating mangoes, and later at the markets we saw vendors selling nothing but mangoes. On the way back to Bishop Kihangire's home, we stopped beyond the Gulu High School to allow the engine time to cool—again. While we waited, we spotted some mothers with their children running toward us with their mangoes. One woman, tall and elegant but practically naked, generously handed me a mango. She had brilliant eyes and a friendly smile, but she looked exhausted and ill fed. Somehow I could sense her despair. As we pulled away in the car, I saw the woman walking toward her home with her hands trying to cover her nakedness from her children. I watched as they turned off towards the remains of a hut that looked as if it had been blown down in a storm. Sadness filled my heart once again. What could I do to help such needy people? I did not have the money or resources to provide all that they needed. Even our struggling government did not have the money to cure this terrible poverty. I think I felt like Moses must have felt when God gave him the task of going to Egypt to set the people free. He replied to

God, "Who am I, that I should go unto Pharaoh, and that I should bring forth the children of Israel out of Egypt?" (Exod 3:11)

I returned to Kampala troubled by the human misery in my country. I was frequently haunted by the vision of that naked woman walking towards her ruined home, a woman who had much dignity but was abused by the formidable foe of poverty.

In December of 1979, I went to America and had the opportunity to appear on the *700 Club*. I spoke of the plight of the widows and children especially in Gulu. From this interview, I received a speaking invitation from Habitat for Humanity in Americus, Georgia. I addressed a large gathering at the Allen Chapel of the African Methodist Episcopal Church. As I spoke, I was especially burdened for that one naked woman in Gulu. After my address, the mayor of Americus made me an honorary citizen of that town. As we spoke together, I realized that he and I shared a common vision. He too saw the necessity of providing decent homes for the women and children in Gulu. In June of 1982, Millard Fuller, the founder of Habitat, visited Uganda to inaugurate the Habitat for Humanity project in Gulu. This same project was later visited by Andrew Young and, at another time, by the daughter of former American president Jimmy Carter.

Rainey Clive came from America as a pioneering worker for the Habitat project. He had worked on a similar project in Zaire and had developed a cordial method of communication with the Africans. They loved and respected him because of the deep compassion he had for our people's situation. With the destruction of so many of the buildings that would provide normal living space, people who came to help were forced to live in temporary huts just as the Gulu people did. I sympathized with anyone from the West who came to serve there. Usually when people talk of crossing cultures in missions, they refer to variations in language, eating habits, music, traditions, and customs. So much more was involved in our situation. Having lived in the West, I realized that people there live in long-established structures, and that it requires a higher sense of accommodation for a person from that culture to operate in an atmosphere in which such structures are nonexistent.

Rainey Clive encountered many problems as a builder in our culture. Before building a house in the West, the builder secures a plan—a blueprint from which he will proceed. In the African tradition, the plan is committed to memory. A builder wakes up one morning and begins to build a house without reference to any plan or design that has been committed to paper. I was amazed at how Clive survived in our nonpaper culture. He became somewhat of a catalyst. He came up with the ideas and gave guidance as the workers jumped in and built the houses. He was very flexible with our culture and did not insist on things being done just his way. As a matter of fact, he worked very well with the local committee, maintaining a spirit of harmony with them.

One day Clive came to visit me in Bakuli and brought pictures of some of the houses that had been built. As he showed me the pictures, he described the families that were the recipients of each house. As he showed me one picture, he described a mother very much like the naked woman I had described to the group in Americus. "Could it be the same woman?" I wondered to myself. Maybe I would never know, but perhaps it was. I often wondered why God had given me such a burden for that one woman and her children. How relieved I would feel to know that that burden had led to a house being provided for her.

Later I was able to travel up to Gulu and see the work that had been accomplished. While there, I was thrilled to find the woman of my burden living in one of the new houses, a house fit for human habitation. I caught a glimpse of God's concern for the poor. Surely he had placed the burden on my heart for this precious family, and he had worked through me to accomplish his will for her. I thanked God for having shown me the needs of the poor and for having given me the compassion and desire to help them. It was through experiences like this that I have come to know more of God's empowering grace. I can declare with boldness and assurance that the same gospel that empowers humans to overcome sin empowers them to overcome poverty.

9

The Karamojong

DYING FOR TAPIOCA ROOT

IN JUNE OF 1980, I took a trip up the eastern section of Uganda, visiting the district authorities to gather information concerning the needs of the people. Unfortunately, I discovered the same problems in every district. People were suffering not only from the ravages of Amin's reign and the Liberation War, but also from the deterioration of society that had been left to itself and was under the darkness of sin. The people were held hostage by the cruel hands of drought, poverty, disorderliness, ignorance, and crime. Sickness, starvation, and death were everywhere.

That year was a particularly disastrous time for the people of Karamoja in northeastern Uganda. A serious drought had hit this area, leaving hundreds of the four million people dead. The death toll from the drought that year exceeded the number of people who had died the previous year during the Liberation War.

Karamoja, boasting one of the most extensive countrysides of open grassland in all of Uganda, is home to many of the nation's cattle keepers. The tall, elegant Karamojong herdsmen, carrying on a long tradition, command hundreds of cattle from which they derive their food, clothing, medicine, dowry, and human dignity. To the Karamojong, ownership of property and cattle determines a man's status in society.

Unfortunately, cattle rustling is also a traditional practice in the area and became even more prevalent after the Liberation War. However, the customary method of raiding with spears gave way to violent and bloody gun battles involving house burning, looting, and raping. During Amin's reign, soldiers took many Karamojong cattle by force. It is believed that in one year, the Karamojong lost over four hundred thousand cows. With the impending drought, many of the Karamojong were reduced to eating leaves and hard seeds that took over six hours to cook.

Famine drove many of the Karamojong in all directions. Some went as far south as Jinja, and others went to Mbale, Sironko, and Soroti. However, wherever they went, they were not received well due to their reputation for their cattle raiding practices.

Once when I was visiting in Sironko (just south of Karamoja), I came upon a Karamojong woman who had been badly speared and was bleeding profusely from her breasts. Bystanders explained to me that the starving woman had been caught stealing tapioca root (cassava) and that she deserved what she had gotten. No one seemed interested in helping her at all. The only one in the area who had a vehicle and could possibly have taken her to the hospital was the district commissioner, but he had no petrol (gasoline), so he was as useless as the others in administering aid. I quickly offered my vehicle to take the dying victim to the hospital. Later the parish chief took me aside to explain further the cultural dilemma: To the people of Sironko, tapioca root is a valuable commodity owned by the property owners of the land on which it grows, but to the Karamojong it is considered a wild plant growing on its own and available to anyone wanting it. There would be no convincing the Karamojong that the woman had stolen anything.

THE BROKEN CROSS

From Sironko we traveled north to Moroto and found similar circumstances. Then the next day we left Moroto for Namalu. Although we were warned that the seventy-mile road from Moroto to Namalu, and the road to Nakapiripirit, were both too dangerous to travel, we determined to continue with our plans and took the roads anyway. Ambushers lay waiting all along the way to plunder whatever goods might be taken. The Red Cross workers confirmed the warning and urged us not to go. On the previous Tuesday, over two thousand armed raiders had stolen about 25,000 head of cattle from Amdat in Karamoja. The raiders had set up roadblocks to thwart any possible interference with their plot. Raiders who would steal cattle would not hesitate to kill anyone who might thwart their plans.

Despite the warnings, we set off in a Land Rover with only Tanzanian police escorts. The route from Moroto to Nakapiripirit was through one continuous savannah. We never saw a single person throughout the way. We did pass by some clusters of homesteads that had belonged to the Karamojong, but they were all deserted, and many were burned to the ground.

We were surprised to find that Nakapiripirit had become a ghost town, but we did speak to a lone Red Cross worker who was also passing through. He warned us to be wary of any person standing along the road. He would probably be a scout for a battalion of raiders nearby. As we continued our journey to Namalo, rather than worrying about snakes or wild animals, we were fearful of sighting any human being.

As we left Nakapiripirit, the terrain changed, with a beautiful mountain range appearing to our left. With the beauty came further threat of a sudden ambush. Tension mounted as we bounced along the hot, dusty roads, surveying the region, heedful of possible impending danger.

Suddenly, as we rounded a corner, we came upon a large truck loaded with cattle. When the driver saw us, he immediately slammed on breaks, bringing the truck to a halt and blocking our way. The cloud of dust that had been following him instantly enveloped the truck, obscuring our view of the truck and of the men. In the distance, we spied a cluster of armed men. Our hearts raced as one of the Tanzanian escorts exclaimed, "We're being ambushed!" and quickly cocked his gun.

I told everyone in the Land Rover to duck down out of sight, and I got out and stood by the vehicle. A van with five soldiers immediately pulled up behind. One called out, "Follow us!"

Hesitantly, I got back into the vehicle and told my escort to drive on. As we moved forward, we watched more soldiers come out of the bushes along the road and jump into the van. Noticing my fear, one of the soldiers walked up to our slow-moving vehicle and quietly informed me, "We are on a mission to rescue cattle stolen from Namalu."

"Well," I thought to myself, "at least we are with the good guys!" That was a small comfort considering we were caught in the middle of a major confrontation between soldiers and cattle rustlers!

As we got closer to the cluster of armed men, we saw that their weapons were automatic guns! We discovered later that they had stolen the guns along with over seven thousand cows after injuring some soldiers at Namalu. Our two vehicles stopped, and both drivers were ordered to lie very low on the ground and to stay out of sight. I gladly joined them. The soldiers, joined by my Tanzanian escorts, moved forward. In a few minutes, I heard the order, "Fire!" followed by a heavy barrage of bullets. The soldiers prevailed. Some of the raiders were killed; others were wounded. The living were all arrested. The cows were recovered and returned to their owners in Namalu.

We arrived in Namalu about noon, somewhat shaken but happy to have survived the morning. However, we were greeted by a different and even more horrible trauma. The place was overflowing with displaced people. Everywhere there was any type of shed, there was a crowd of people. In Moroto, I had been told to find Brother Fortumato and Sister Jin Franca, who were the organizers of the feeding center in the area. We spied a humble Catholic church across the way and began making our way toward it, passing masses of naked, starving, and emaciated people. It was a frightening and distressing experience. One young girl, suspecting we were looking for the Catholic fathers, came to us and pointed to the church. "Papa gone to prayers," she informed us. By her side was another heartbreaking sight. A little girl, completely emaciated with eyes sunken and bones protruding, stood seemingly oblivious to the flies crawling on her lips and competing to scoop out her eyeballs. I suddenly understood why the fathers had retreated from this nightmare to pray.

From a distance, I saw a father come out of the church led by a man that I suspected might be Brother Fortumato. I actually guessed right; it was Brother Fortumato. He greeted me warmly as if he knew me. Actually, he had been informed by radio that I was coming and had eagerly anticipated my arrival. He introduced me to the Catholic missionaries who had come from the Diocese of Gulu and were busy preparing porridge in a huge container. The porridge provided a faint smell of hope in the midst of despair and death.

As if the scene of starving people were not horrendous enough, Brother Fortumato explained that thirty children were dying right there at the feeding center every day. As I watched the starving people line up for their meager ration of porridge, I realized that there were three additional lines of new arrivals.

He warned me, "As the new arrivals begin to eat, don't be surprised to see some falling down dead even after taking the porridge, for some are already too dehydrated to live." He continued in a whisper: "The hyenas in the area are so full that they are no longer eating the dead bodies." Before he finished the sentence, an old man had dropped dead. Sadly, the man was the father of Lokiru, a young boy who was traveling with me. There was no commotion, as death had become the norm.

As I listened to Brother Fortumato, my eyes fell upon one woman sitting in the dust with several other mothers who were feeding their infants with crumbs they had collected from the garbage dumps. This particular woman had a ragged piece of cloth wrapped around her waist, and around her neck hung a broken cross. She had a slight cut across her right cheek, and on her lap were a few dry cassava peelings not much different in color from her soiled loincloth. Her children, sitting in a semicircle, were just staring into their mother's face. As she began breaking the peeling into smaller pieces, one child picked up a piece and was about to eat it. The mother slapped her hand until the peeling fell onto the ground. The starving child cried furiously, but the mother seemed to ignore her. When she was finished, she and her children closed their eyes; the woman gave a word of thanks, and then distributed the broken pieces to her children.

I was dumbfounded by all that was going on around me. Evidently, God wanted me to see this scenario, but it was completely overwhelming. There was the shock of the old man lying on the grass dead, and in my mind I was torn apart about what to say to Lokiru when I returned to the car to tell him that his father had just died. At the same time, I had to remain polite and listen to Brother Fortumato's narration of the situation.

My heart could take no more. I said goodbye to the fathers, and the parish chief escorted me to the car. As we drove away, I found myself gazing into the skies. I wanted to see Jesus, for I had so many questions to ask. As I pondered, a sermon that I had preached many times wormed its way once again into my heart. Jesus had taken the five loaves and the two fish, looked up into heaven and given thanks. He then broke the paltry amount of food and fed five thousand people. Like Jesus, the woman had given thanks for something that was not enough. The Spirit spoke to my heart: "You do likewise."

A CRY FROM THE DYING

At Mbale, I received an urgent message informing me of a camp near Ngega where two thousand Karamojong were starving. We left immediately with a police escort. My first glimpse of the camp was a long line of graves. In the faces of the people that had gathered there, I saw death. One of the elders spoke to me: "We are not sick, but death drips from us.

We are terrified to sleep because in the morning, many remain in eternal sleep. Every night we are visited by the silence of death. Soon we will all sleep here." With this statement he pointed to the sky. "There is no candle to light," he continued, "no door to lock, no roof to shelter us. But the depth of the grave is the same length as the distance to the source that gives us moonlight at night. We are like the stars which disappear at sunrise."

While he was speaking, five women stood in front of me. As he finished, they pulled the skin of their stomachs out. One of them spoke. "This was once a mother's womb. See, now it is dead rubber. In it I bore children who have been eaten by the grave. This stomach was their first grave."

A man stood up, and in his arms he held his emaciated seven-year-old son, whom I now know as Okiru Ladat. That morning the boy's mother had died of starvation. He did not say a word, and there was complete silence all around. Not looking at me, he said to the people, "Listen to the silence and you will hear death counting us to know our number."

Then he turned to me and said, "What is killing us is not starvation but silence. Our neighbors the Sebei are silent. Our neighbors the Bagisu are silent. Our neighbors the Acholi are silent. When we have cattle; they are not silent. They invade us, but now we have no cattle, and they are silent, and we are no more." I thought then of the Good Samaritan and wished to touch this man's suffering with Christ's love. He stumbled because of his weariness. Soon he was near enough to touch me, and he threw the child to me with the words, "Take him to those who are silent."

Then I knew I must take all the children I could persuade to come with me from here and from Mbale. I managed to gather thirty-two. Among them were Okiru Ladat, and Madanda, a boy I had seen that morning at the Mbale bus park lying in the dust, too weary to run away. The transport for the thirty-two children was an open Land Rover. I told them of the dangers, but they were undaunted. One suggested that they would pretend they were ex-convicts, and everyone would be frightened of them. In their humor, I saw hope. I realized that the hope that they needed must be a permanent hope, not merely food for a day and shelter for a night. God had seen this need and, unknown to me, had already provided an answer to my prayers. In his infinite wisdom and love, he was already preparing people and facilities for a home for these orphans.

Yea, though I walk through the valley of the shadow of death, I will fear no evil: for thou art with me; thy rod and thy staff they comfort me. Thou preparest a table before me in the presence of mine enemies: thou anointest my head with oil: my cup runneth over. (Ps 23:4–5)

10

The Farm Projects

LUKUMBI AND GARY BAJUS

IN MAY 1980, MUWANGA had become chairman of the military commission and had allocated a number of farms to Africa Foundation. The abandoned farms were overgrown and neglected. The first farm, allocated in June 1980, was a two-thousand-acre farm at Lukumbi, near Jinja and close to the electricity dam on the Nile. The farm had been seized from a previous owner by one of Amin's ministers. On July 5, 1980, Allan Smith, Richard Nsubuga, and I went to Lukumbi and took over the farm. Our first act was to hold a service under a tree to thank God for yet another wonderful provision.

I took Gary Bajus, an American volunteer who had come to Uganda to assist with the work of Africa Foundation, to the farm, but I was not sure whether he could survive in a rural setting as rugged as this. I wondered how he would function among the people of a different culture. I left him at the farm with only a thin blanket in a house that had very poor ventilation. When I visited the farm the following week, I was surprised to see chairs and furniture. He nonchalantly explained to me that the neighbors had returned the items they had looted in Amin's time. Obviously Gary had great skill in working with the people of a different culture if, in the period of just one week, he had been able to meet the neighbors and build such a friendly relationship with them that they willingly returned the furniture they had stolen. I was amazed at the finesse of the American, and thrilled at the marvelous working of the hand of God who had provided in such an amazing way.

In October 1980, I received bad news. Gary was ill with a throat infection, and it seemed certain that he would die. Immediately, I rushed to his side. He still had one thin blanket. He had given the rest of his possessions to those whom he saw as needier than himself. I asked him to come back to Kampala with me for a chance to rest and recover, but he stubbornly refused. I even threatened to bring the police to force him to leave the farm. Although he could barely speak due to pain and weakness, he managed to whisper his response. "You may bring the army, but I am not moving." In desperation, I told him he was going to die if he did not come with me, but he mouthed his argument, "When the people become sick here, they die here. I want to die with them, and you can bury me where they are buried." I saw then why the people had loved him, for they had seen God's love and caring in his actions. I knew this must be the same faith as of that of the prophets of old. Just as God had called Moses to the Israelites, he had called Gary Bajus to the people of Uganda. A new ray of strength developed in me arising from the testimony of this great man.

I left Gary on the farm that day, no longer afraid in my heart. He soon recovered and continued attending to the displaced children, the widowed mothers, and the sick. Gary never judged his ability in terms of his formal education, and this humble attitude freed him to serve. He told me that he based his ministry on Psalm 78:72, a verse that was read at his ordination. "So he fed them according to the integrity of his heart; and guided them by the skillfulness of his hands."

At one time there was no electricity at Lukumbi, and with over eight hundred children to care for, a lack of power was a major hindrance. Gary shared the dilemma with a friend who suggested that he use the methane from the children's feces to generate power.

Gary creatively turned a tank into a pit latrine, and when it was full, he closed the tank, leaving two outlets. Using the contraption, he was able to generate enough power to light several rooms. When the children went to bed around ten o'clock the first night, Gary closed the outlets and the lights went off. Around two thirty the next morning, the area was rocked by a loud boom. It sounded as if an atomic bomb had detonated. Silence followed the explosion, but then the children erupted in hysterical laughter. The tank had exploded, sending feces raining upon everything in sight. Creative Gary had overlooked one valuable point in his invention. He had left no outlet for the ever-building gas to escape. That was the end of that experiment!

Being from the West, Gary enjoyed taking on the persona of a cowboy. He was tough, and no one wanted to tangle with him. He frequently used the phrase, "A cowboy never dies," and the children would laugh. They soon began to call him *the cowboy who never dies*. They even took the phrase as a theme for their own lives.

One day I found a boy eating a piece of fish from the garbage. I reminded him that people often put poison on fish to kill rats, and I asked, "Aren't you afraid of being poisoned by eating that?"

He responded smartly, "A cowboy never dies." I knew immediately that this boy had been in one of our homes.

THE NAMALU FARM

In late 1980, the director of the International Christian Aid, Joe Baas, came to my office with a group of people from West Germany looking for a program in Uganda that needed assistance. During the Second World War, the Americans had rendered great assistance to the people who were trapped in East Germany. To show their gratitude to America, these West Germans wanted to assist the people of Uganda who had suffered from the tyranny of Idi Amin, just as the Germans had suffered at the hands of Adolf Hitler.

I shared with Joe Baas the prospect of turning the farm at Namalu into a site of hope. The farm, another allocation to the Africa Foundation, had at one time been a prosperous government farm covering several miles of land in Karamoja. Due to Amin's years of misrule and mismanagement, the farm had deteriorated and was no longer in use by anyone.

My experience in Karamoja had taught me that it would not be easy to change the cultural attitudes of the people toward education. As a matter of fact, the ancestors of the present Karamojong had been so opposed to education that they had held a special ceremony, placing a pen nib symbolizing education into a coffin and burying it as a sign of their hostility toward any form of foreign teaching. In order truly to help these people, we would have to convince them to accept some type of education, so that they could support themselves. Handouts of food, clothing, and shelter would be temporary bandages without the acquisition of skills.

We decided first of all to use food as payment for work. When the people agreed to work, they would be forced to acquire some basic skills. Also, they would experience the intrinsic rewards that come with a job accomplished. I suggested, too, that children be gathered at Namalu and given a positive orientation toward education. These children, as agents of change, could then return to their homes and communities in Karamoja and share their newly found values and knowledge.

In a matter of just a few weeks, a jet loaded with medical equipment, food, tents, and school supplies from West Germany landed at Entebbe Airport, and the project at Namalu was begun. Several months later, the head of the project invited me to visit Namalu. My eyes saw what I did not expect. The farm had been turned into a glamorous place, teaming with children and teenagers from all over Karamoja who were working, learning, and growing in a positive environment.

Again to my surprise and utter amazement, my eyes saw what God wanted me to see—that same woman with the broken cross and the scar on her cheek. She and her three children had been recipients of good clothing.

"Amazing grace, how sweet the sound . . . "

11

Akarun Akalam (Unearthing the Pen)

A T THE TIME THAT I was appointed chairman of the National Council for Children, the Save the Children Organizations from the United Kingdom, Norway, and Denmark were merging to create the new Save the Children Fund of Uganda. They called the organization Red Banner, and one of their main goals was to introduce formal education in Karamoja. They made several unsuccessful attempts before they finally introduced an alternative approach that they called *Abek*.

Since schooling was perceived by the Karamojong as something that undermined their cultural traits, which were necessary for their survival, Red Banner came to realize that they must develop a program that would fit the cultural and economic demands of the people and support their traditions. Abek was designed to follow the movements of the Karamojong, who were migrant herdsmen constantly in search of grass and water for their cattle. The people were taught skills that would easily mesh with their traditions rather than alter their culture.

Aina Bergstrom, a Red Banner representative from Norway, told me an interesting story revealing the source of the Karamojong's aversion to education. This story about the Jie tribe in Karamoja was later confirmed to me by different Karamojong elders.

The failure of Jie children to succeed in school is blamed by the Jie today on the actions of their forefathers. With the outbreak of war with Germany in 1939, the colonial authorities apparently tried unsuccessfully to recruit Jie youths to join the King's East African Rifles. Their refusal was met with force, and some people were arrested and later died in prison, and others were said to have been shot for desertion.

The pen was seen as an instrument of oppression and became the focus of Jie resentment because it was used to register the names of recruits. The recruiters forced the young men to cut off the traditional headdress of matted hair (*atokot*), so the recruitment pen was also associated with this violent and often bloody shearing. Besides the forced recruitment of Jie youth into the army, vaccination of animals was also looked upon with great suspicion. The Jie saw it as a move by the colonial leadership to maliciously exterminate their animals. The tribe had had no previous experience with vaccination and therefore met it with strong resistance.

Seeing their sons so cruelly mistreated by the British soldiers, the Jie elders decided to take action. Alinga, a prominent elder of the Ng'ikotido clan, planned and executed a special ceremony in the sacred grove of their clan. They put a curse on education, and to symbolize the curse, they offered a black ox as a sacrifice and buried a pen nib. They saw immediate "results" from their curse, as one hundred of their riflemen were sent home with an "incurable" eye disease that then miraculously cleared up.

It is believed that their curse has persisted to thwart the efforts of contemporary Jie young people to succeed in education. Recently, the generation following those who made the curse felt it was time to *tongaathi ngidwe*—open up the way for the children. They asked the elders to lift the curse so that their children could succeed at school, and so that Jie graduates could rise to office and better represent Jie interests in government. To achieve this goal, they formed the Jie Country Educational Lobby Group, which requested the elders to "unearth the pen."

The unearthing ceremony took place in November 1995. The sons of the men who had originally conducted the ceremony reenacted their fathers' roles. Elders from all seven Jie clans participated and made appeals to God for the lifting of the curse. They offered many prayers for the betterment of the Jie. The elders slept at the site, and by morning the curse was thought to have been lifted. The elders have agreed to return and monitor the effects of "unearthing the pen" annually, to ensure that the curse truly was annulled.

The experience of this ritual was the dawning of recognition among the adults of the Jie-Karamojong of the importance of education. They realized that the future would bring change and possible exploitation of their traditional lands. With proper education, their children would be equipped to handle the challenges and to protect their society and way of life.

The Karamojong had a strong sense of cultural identity and solidarity and a vast body of indigenous knowledge. They also held their elders in high esteem. In 1980, I was among a delegation of government leaders who went to Karamoja. I observed that whenever we held a meeting, the Karamojong never seemed to listen to any of us. They were occupied with their sniffing and sneezing and being amused with themselves. When one of us would ask a general question that required an affirmative response, the Karamojong would all look toward a similar direction. Later I was told that each cluster of people would first get the proper response from their elder. If he nodded affirmatively, they would also do the same.

At the end of each speech, a person from the crowd would first cross-examine the speaker, verifying specific statements he had made. Then the Karamojong would raise questions about the topics he had verified in the exact order that he had presented them. It was amazing that the questioner was able to reproduce the speaker's statements verbatim after apparently having not paid attention at all.

The children were no different from the adults of the tribes, in that they had almost photographic minds. In 1980, I was invited as chief guest to a graduation ceremony held at a convent near Moroto Town. Among the thirty graduates, there were just two Karamojong. The rest of the students were from the neighboring tribes of Iteso, Acholi, and Kumi. The principal told me that the Karamojong students coming to that institution were extremely brilliant, but that they did not study for certificates. He explained that they were keen to study chemistry and physics, but as soon as they learned to make gunpowder and guns, they abandoned the college. In a way, they wanted knowledge to improve their own knowledge, but they did not want knowledge that would take away their indigenous beliefs.

Every time I went to Karamoja, I brought back with me three to five children who had lost their parents. Before the end of 1980, I had collected over forty-five children. Phillip Omanik, whose mother and father had both starved to death, was one of those children. In the Karamojong homesteads, there is always an elder who is the leader of all the people. Subconsciously Phillip acted like an elder among the Karamojong children. The children would always consult with him before making any decision.

Among the forty-five children were fifteen girls. Their first home was Lukumbi Farm. One day Phillip informed me that we were losing one or two girls every night. To the Karamojong, the dowry was more important than the education of a daughter. A girl's parents could profit more from marrying her off than from educating her, so adult Karamojong from Jinja Town would frequent the farm to smuggle these girls out in order to allow their families to marry them off. Our watchman, also a Karamojong, conveniently overlooked the abductions. How disappointing it was that, despite all our efforts to instill the importance of education into the people of Karamoja, they were bound by their deep-rooted customs and misplaced values!

Along with our many disappointments, we also enjoyed some outstanding successes. Phillip was one of those triumphs. His life was changed drastically at the home as he came to know Christ and grew spiritually strong. He completed his studies in agriculture at Eldoret in Kenya and, with several other boys, returned to Karamoja to introduced farming in their hometown of Iriri. Phillip and the other men now teach Sunday school classes and farming skills to neighboring villages. Phillip undertook theological studies and has started a church in Karamoja. He is happily married, and even named his firstborn Kefa. His life is evidence of the power of the Word of God to change lives.

> Therefore shall ye lay up these my words in your heart and in your soul, and bind them for a sign upon your hand, that they may be as frontlets between your eyes. And ye shall teach them to your children, speaking of them when thou sittest in thine house, and when thou walkest by the way, when thou liest down, and when thou risest up. And thou shalt write them upon the door posts of thine house, and upon thy gates: That your days may be multiplied, and the days of your children, in the land which the LORD sware unto your fathers to give them, as the days of heaven upon the earth. (Deut 11:18–21)

12

The Shoe Box

I DON'T REMEMBER WHOSE idea it was, but what a great blessing the children of America were to the children in our homes! Some creative individual came up with the idea of using simple shoe boxes filled with necessities to minister to our children. The program worked something like a pen-pal arrangement and was a powerful tool in communication and building bridges across cultures, and even served to plant seeds for missions in the hearts of the American children who participated.

In this arrangement, a child abroad would be encouraged to put into an empty shoe box items like toiletries, socks, a pen, toothpaste, a toothbrush, a small T-shirt, a simple dress, soap, and a small Bible. In addition, the sender would include in the box a photo and a brief letter. Having properly closed the box, the sender would address it to a child of his or her age and send it to Africa Foundation, P. O. Box 4100, Kampala, Uganda. Between 1981 and 1994, we received over a hundred boxes a month. The child who received each box would write a thank-you letter to the sender, and then as a sign of great pride, he would hang the photo of the sender at his bedside. The picture became somewhat of a status symbol for the child who displayed it. Thus it became a matter of great concern for those children who lacked a sender's photo. The contents of the shoe box helped a great deal, especially with the essential commodities necessary for civilized life, but the letters and photos made the children feel loved and important, and symbolized the hope beyond their past, and a connection to a brighter future.

Soon after the program began, I came across a delightful letter from a boy of six from Rye, New Hampshire. The boy was eager to have an orphaned child in Uganda as a pen pal and wrote a most delightful and cheerful letter.

Dear Kefa,

My name is John. I am six. I want a pen pal in Uganda, an orphan.
We have five in my family, my mom, dad, a dog, a cat, and me.
Outside we have good flowers.

Sincerely,

John

Of course, the six-year-old boy who received the letter and box was
delighted. He showed the letter to an eight-year-old friend, who read it
and burst into laughter. "What do a dog and a cat have to do with John's
family?" he queried.

Similarly, our children revealed a definite cultural gap in their letters
back to the Americans. Sometimes they made shocking requests, as did
Kato in his letter.

I am eight years old and my name is Kato. Please send me one
motorcycle, a helicopter, and a Land Rover.

Such were the cultural misconceptions that needed to be rectified in
the shoe box of cultural exchange.

There was a time when Moammar Gadaffi came to Uganda and
spoke disparagingly of America in a televised speech. During that particular weekend, I was at the farm in Lukumbi. I was dumbfounded to spy
a band of about sixty small children outside my room holding leaves and
stomping their feet as if they were an army of the Lord. They marched in
unison and waved the leaves. I was curious to know what all the stomping
was about, so they eagerly explained, "It is against the man Gadaffi. He
spoke bad things about our shoe-box friends in America."

Of course, I wanted to know what adult was behind this demonstration. Certainly I could not allow our children to be exploited as political
pawns. However, they quickly assured me that no adult had told them to
express any opinions. They had initiated the demonstration themselves
out of devotion to the children represented by the photos beside their
beds.

Would that we all had the innocence of childhood! If we were as
devoted to our heavenly Father in appreciation for his marvelous gift
of salvation as the children were to total strangers who had sent them a
few trinkets, we would be turning the world upside down for Christ. If a

simple shoe box can bind the hearts of strangers, should not the greatest gift bind our hearts to the Creator who loves us as his children?

> Verily I say unto you, Except ye be converted, and become as little children, ye shall not enter into the kingdom of heaven. (Matt 18:3)

13

The Slums

BY 1982 THERE WERE fewer street children living on the streets of Kampala, but the slums were jammed with hundreds of children who had nothing to do. Potential street children or "part-timers," as they were called, loitered in the streets during the day but returned to their family units at night. The major slum areas, clustered within Kampala City, were packed with impoverished individuals who had no hope and were operating with a slum mentality.

In one slum area, Kisenyi, there were over 48,000 families with an average of five to seven children per family. A family, usually with only one parent, would be jammed into a small room of five by seven feet with little or no furniture; tattered, filthy linens; possibly a charcoal stove; and sooty walls. Most of the pit latrines were either broken or overfilled, so any type of sanitation was nonexistent. The people suffered from malnutrition and health issues of all kinds. Within the nine years of Amin's misrule and terror, the slums had been reduced to absurdity. In addition, over the previous ten-year period, the population in the slums had doubled, further exacerbating the penury of the people.

Through each slum ran a channel which people used as a toilet and at the same time for bathing, further spreading sickness and disease. Most of the bathing shades had been broken down, and women would wash without adequate privacy. The incidents of rape and child defilement were rampant in the slum areas of Makerere, Kivulu, Kesenyi, Wabigalo, and Kifumbira of Kamwokya. Amin's soldiers had wreaked havoc in this area, establishing a mentality of disrespect for human life, which continued even after the soldiers were removed.

The poverty in the slum areas was not just a lack of material possessions. It was a formidable demonic force intended to dehumanize God's beautiful creation. Wickedness prevailed, and the people were in the clutches of a totally godless existence. Bound by their sin, poverty, ignorance, and helplessness, they could not even imagine a hope for the future and a better life. All they could do was to wallow in their misery.

In Africa Foundation, we resolved to tackle this demonic force through the power and love of God. We began with intense prayer, claiming God's promise found in James 5:16: "Confess your faults one to another, and pray one for another, that ye may be healed. The effectual fervent prayer of a righteous man availeth much." We prayed not only for the people and their needs, but also for our own strength and wisdom as we sought to effect a change. We prayed that as we reached out and met physical needs in the name of Christ, God would tenderize the hearts of individuals and make them receptive to the gospel, which is, of course, the ultimate healing factor in any situation.

How could people living in such an environment be empowered to overcome the chains of abject poverty? Christ is the ultimate answer, but we had to find a way to show them his love. We realized that we had to begin with changing their mindset. Their thinking deformed their bodies, forcing a stagnant, repugnant lifestyle. Women and young girls had the lowest self-image of all the people, and many had given their lives to prostitution as a sign of despair. The men did the odd jobs. They were wheelbarrow pushers, hawkers, shoe shiners, car cleaners, truck loaders—not that there was anything wrong with such jobs. There was no choice for other opportunities in such a destitute society. Some of the families had lived in the slums for generations. Girls followed the examples of their mothers, selling their bodies for a meager sum just to survive. If a mother ever found one of her customers fondling her daughter, the mother would chop the daughter's face so that no man would ever be attracted to her again.

Girls got pregnant at the age of thirteen, and it was such girls who aborted their babies. They did not want pregnancy to get in the way of their business. Several times we found babies thrown into pit latrines, on garbage dumps, in gutters, and along the Nakivubo stream. We rescued these unwanted babies, and in 1982, began a baby department at the children's home at Mukono Dandira.

We targeted the children as agents of change because we felt they would be moldable and amenable to new ideas and then in turn would influence their families. In 1982, our workers surveyed the slums and sampled over eight hundred families who were absolutely desperate or despondent. From each of these homes, the workers selected one child for support. This child was entitled to the same treatment as the children in our homes. The child received a blanket, soap, medical care, and tuition fee. We then encouraged these children to be a channel of support to their families by sharing the blanket and soap with siblings. This plan supported the African concept of the extended family and helped to build a sense of unity and responsibility. Helping one child in a family won us a position of respect in the family, and the parents would listen to our advice and teaching. We had an exceptional opportunity to minister to mothers. Ladies came in large numbers to our workshops on such topics as family planning, home improvement, and sanitation. No matter what the topic was, we were able to share with the women about the love of God and his wonderful plan for their salvation.

Nansubuga, a single mother of six children, lived on the outskirts of the slum right along the Nakivubo Channel. For some reason our workers had selected two of her children to receive benefits from Africa Foundation, although the rule was for only one child per family to be chosen. Nansubuga often invited me to visit her home, and one afternoon, I agreed to accompany her there. She was a unique lady in that she was cheerful and talkative and always did her best to be properly groomed and clean. As we walked together, she explained to me that her husband had been a mechanic but had been killed just before the Liberation War. As we neared her home, a small, previously abandoned shack, her children burst into a boisterous welcome. Broken car parts littered the area around the hovel, a strange black dog lay in the yard, and some spotted clothes hung on the line. Two cassava roots were roasting on the fireplace outside, and I wondered how two measly roots could feed a family of seven. As we approached the door, Nansubuga's face began to register some signs of depression. Inside, the sitting room was furnished with old car seats that had been reduced to naked wires. The sitting room and bedroom were flooded with that foul-smelling water oozing from the channel. Her countenance quickly changed from her usual cheerful personality, and she burst into loud sobbing. She began lamenting over the loss of her husband who had been shot dead in that very room. The children, seeing their mother weeping, came and knelt in the debris beside her and joined in wailing for their father who had been dead for four years.

I was dumbfounded. Suddenly I felt the grief, hopelessness, and suffering that was all around me. I hated the poverty and human misery that seemed to engulf the world, and I loathed the regime that had aggravated an already pitiful existence. I wanted so desperately to reach out and fix all their problems, but I felt helpless against such extreme destitution. I stood frozen, wondering what to do or say. This family needed to be reassured, but I did not have anything to offer as an immediate solution. I comforted them the best that I could and pledged that we would continue to pay school fees for two of the children.

When Nansubuga composed herself, she invited me to sit down. I sat on the fragments of the car seat while the children sang two songs for me. The cheerful singing was good therapy for my broken heart. I realized that Nansubuga's jolly exterior was a cushion to pad the misery of her life and the inward bleeding of her heart.

As I walked away that day, I prayed to God to help me to minister to the hurting hearts and lives all around me. I have learned by experience not to rush to conclusions, and I use two verses from Ecclesiastes as guides in circumstances that lend themselves to hopelessness: "Be not rash with thy mouth, and let not thine heart be hasty to utter any thing before God: for God is in heaven, and thou upon earth: therefore let thy words be few" (Eccl 5:2); and "Suffer not thy mouth to cause thy flesh to sin; neither say thou before the angel, that it was an error: wherefore should God be angry at thy voice, and destroy the work of thine hands?" (Eccl 5:6).

Human anger cannot work out God's righteousness; but being human, I always catch myself falling short of patience. Consequently I must take time to pray and be protected against a spirit of bitterness. I know that there is great power in the gospel—"Therefore I take pleasure in infirmities, in reproaches, in necessities, in persecutions, in distresses for Christ's sake: for when I am weak then am I strong" (2 Cor 12:10). It is not my strength then, but the power of God working in me.

Later on, this family experienced the joy of being born again, and with much patience Nansubuga's daughters completed their education, got jobs, and bought a house for their mother. The girls are all married and lead good lives.

14

The Beggars

A NEW IDEA

IN MY DEALINGS WITH the children, I came into daily contact with more and more beggars, prostitutes, and lepers; with the halt, the lame, and the blind. As I helped the children, I wondered whether there was any way I could help these people, too. In the West, trying to persuade people to go work in Uganda, I was often asked if any professional qualifications were required. I always replied that the qualification was simple: It was love. I was not referring to the celluloid love of Hollywood but to the love of a Gary Bajus: love in word and deed. The children had been turned into a family, but what could I give the beggars to bring meaning to their lives?

During the Liberation War, the beggars had left the city, but by 1982 they had returned, particularly on the verandas of the then-vacated Barclay's Bank, on Janaan Street, on Luwumu Street, on William Street, and at the bus park. On March 20, 1982, I decided to call a meeting of the beggars at the Kampala bus park. At that meeting, I invited them to come to the Africa Foundation so that together we could plan what to do to improve their situations. We decided that a workshop would be an excellent beginning, and so the following Saturday, more than 150 beggars converged at the Foundation. I needed desperately to gain insight into their needs, philosophies, and ways of thinking, so I employed the artistry in me. I gave each person paper, paint, and brushes and asked them to portray on paper their perception of the world. I hoped that the paintings would tell us what they could not put into words. They quickly began working quietly, paying no attention to my coming and going. The results were astonishing.

I had asked my secretary to record the events of this meeting, but after ten minutes, she passed me a note saying that she was ill and needed to leave. Of course, I agreed. When the workshop was over, I went to my office to find her still there. I was surprised to find that she had not gone home. She explained that she was not ill but pregnant and that she was afraid that if she stayed and looked at the ugly sights of the deformed beggars, she would produce a deformed baby. The sight of the beggars was indeed grotesque, but the smell was just as horrible. These people never washed. Some had long, soiled hair, and others had twisted faces with half shaven heads painted with blood. Some appeared to have infected wounds on their faces, hands, and chests. Some of the women had small children whom they used as begging pets.

The women produced mostly decorative patterns, but the men painted solid images. One man painted a picture of water lilies and later explained that the secret of a happy life was found in floating as a water lily floats. Another man painted a bold red circle, and inside it he drew a human being in the form of a lizard. His picture reminded me of the aboriginal paintings I had seen in Australia. I asked him what it meant, and he told me that the world is like a ball in which humanity is being squeezed. I was amazed at his ability and asked him whether he was aware of his talent for painting. He did not answer me.

I had invited Eli Kyeyune, a prominent artist, to be an external examiner, and he selected the painting of the lizard as the best of all the paintings. When Eli left, the man who had painted that winning picture called me aside to speak to me where no one could hear. We walked over to a corner of the room where the man proceeded to show me a terrible wound on his right leg that was so deep that the bones were visible. "I am not a beggar," he explained. "I live among the beggars because they feed me. I am a beggar among the beggars, for they are better than me. They have a will to live, but I yearn only for death. I sit in the rain hoping I will catch a fever and die. There is not a day I do not yearn for death. Why do you tell me that I have talent? I have nothing, and you will not allow me to die in peace. Why do you make me to suffer?"

I do not remember what I said to him, but when I finished, he stared at me for a long time. Then he spoke. "Can you get me money to return to the hospital to have my wound healed?"

The Beggars

In less than a week, eleven beggars with chronic diseases returned to the hospital for treatment. All went willingly, convinced of a new sense of their own worth after realizing their talents in art.

At their first meeting, the beggars had elected a chairman, Hamzat Nvule. Nvule was a leper who had lost a leg, his nose, and all his fingers due to the disease. The beggars had, however, chosen wisely. Nvule had a brilliant mind, the qualities of leadership, and even a photographic memory. He was among those who went to the hospital and returned with a certificate to show that he had completed his full course of leprosy treatment.

Nvule explained to me what it meant to be a beggar. He himself owned a piece of land at Nyenga, where he also had a wife and children. Every Friday, he went home to his family. He explained that the beggars knew each other by name and knew to which camp each beggar belonged. They identified themselves as Barclays, William Street, or bus park members. Each had his own territory, and no beggar interfered with another's place of begging.

Nvule advised that we should make materials available to enable the beggars to discover their hidden talents in such areas as handicrafts, basketry, weaving, carving, tailoring, and shoe making and repairing. They would come each day to the workshop and produce products to be sold. Nvule also advised that, in addition to food, I should give a small financial reward. So every beggar who came to the workshops received one meal a day and, at the end of each day, was given 250 Ugandan shillings. The pay was enough to buy a kilo of sugar, a kilo of meat, or two or three very large pieces of soap.

Unfortunately, a problem soon developed. The word had gotten out that the Africa Foundation was giving out money and free food, and people who were not true beggars began showing up in droves. It was Nvule who found the solution. He suggested that I announce publicly that we were no longer giving money at the end of the day. Soon only the beggars remained. Nvule, who knew the true beggars, continued to distribute money each night to those who had worked in the shop during the day.

I was puzzled by the fact that the workshop was empty every Friday. Nvule explained to me that the Moslems had a belief that giving alms to beggars on Fridays would secure the salvation of the almsgiver. It was definitely more profitable for the beggars to be on the streets that day than weaving or painting in the workshop! I had been encouraging the public

71

to stop throwing money to the beggars and to begin thinking of projects that would make the beggars self-reliant. Now I realized that the religion of many of the people was actually promoting the begging lifestyle.

THE HUTTERIANS

Early in our ministry to the beggars, I visited the Hutterian Brethren in America. The group, a branch of Anabaptists similar to the Amish and Mennonites, live a simple lifestyle and hold to a strong sense of community life. I went to America to seek their guidance, hoping to discover some creative ideas to incorporate into the lives of the indigent Ugandans. I was met at the airport by Hans Meier and other brothers, who took me to Woodcrest, where I was greeted with love and friendship. The people were eager to know about my work, so I enthusiastically outlined to them the needs of the Ugandan beggars.

That evening I had dinner with over four hundred members of the community. After the meal, I was invited to attend the brotherhood meeting. This was a great honor for me, for it is there that the members meet and decide together the major issues and concerns of the community. I shared with the brothers the story that Jesus told of the man who, when he received a friend at night, had nothing to put before him. I related closely to that man, as I had nothing to put before 150 beggars in Uganda.

At the meeting, Christopher Arnold, the community leader, put a proposal to the brotherhood to look into the needs of these 150 beggars. It was decided to send immediate relief. The brothers shared the need with the other surrounding communities, and they all voted unanimously to support our ministry to the beggars. The same night the brotherhood agreed to send a container of relief goods to Uganda as soon as possible. My heart overflowed with joy when they shared with me their decision.

Gradually, I learned more of how the brotherhood operated. Hans Meier explained to me that all worked for the common good of the community. No member drew a salary, but each received according to his need. I wondered how the beggars would respond to such a concept and resolved to raise this issue with them upon my return.

I felt it would be best to broach the issue in my Bible studies with the beggars, as it was definitely a scriptural practice. In one evening study, we looked at Acts 4:32, which says, "And the multitude of them that believed were of one heart and of one soul: neither said any of them that ought of the things which he possessed was his own; but they had all things common." We also read Acts 4:35: "And laid them down at the apostles' feet: and distribution was made unto every man according as he had need."

I asked them what they thought these verses meant. One member insisted the passage meant that if one of them had a bicycle, that all must have bicycles since they all had to have things in common. That answer brought laughter from the others. Another said that each had a different need: one may want a bicycle; another may not, while those without legs to ride a bicycle or walk may need a wheelchair. Some would need neither, but fees for their children's schooling, while those without children had no school fees to pay.

At this point, I interrupted and pointed out that even in the Foundation, the needs of each member were different. The general manager had four children, while the lady who serves the tea had six. Yet the salary of the manager was three times greater. I then asked them to question the whole idea of salaries, especially in the family of Africa Foundation. The arguments went back and forth, and finally, Hamzat Nvule spoke:

> "For many years I have been begging to keep my family and to pay for my children's schooling. Yet now I and my family live better in the love of the Foundation than many who are paid salaries every month. Let us receive according to our needs, and let us all respond to the needs of each individual member."

The members then passed a resolution that from henceforth, the new community, the family of beggars, would each receive according to his needs rather than a set amount for all. This new policy not only provided for the necessities of the members, but fostered love and a compassionate attitude among the group. They learned to resist greed and to be concerned about each other in a new and fresh fashion.

The Hutterians' forty-foot container soon arrived. It was filled with farming implements, used clothing, and many tools for making and repairing shoes. We occupied a shop on Luwumu Street where the women made sweaters and the men made shoes, wallets, belts, and many other leather items. A committee set up by the beggars themselves, under the chairmanship of Hamzat Nvule, monitored the income and deposited all the money into a bank account.

By the end of 1982, the beggars had a great deal of money in the account. With the clothes and bedding that came in the Hutterian containers, the image of the beggars changed tremendously. After all, they now had the most profitable project in town!

At the end of the year, they divided the proceeds "as each person had need." Over one hundred of them returned to their communities of origin. Money was designated to each individual to buy a plot of land and to build a small house. Those who had homes with thatched roofs turned them into metal roofs. They were encouraged to grow food and cash crops. By mid-1983, they were running their own projects. Only five beneficiaries, including Hamzat, remained in the city, and the project came to a close.

A FAILED EXPERIMENT

Another benefit that we received from our relationship with the Hutterians came in the form of a creative worker. The Hutterian community from England sent a young man named Simeon to help with children of Africa Foundation. Simeon became houseparent for the older boys at Moneko Farm. He worked well and was very tough on discipline.

Simeon suggested that since street children had such well-built bodies, we should try them out in boxing. I had no objection to the boys' learning a new sport, so Simeon hired a trainer. Their first fight was at Kayunga between the police and the children of the Foundation. The occasion attracted almost the whole town of Kayunga. Ayub boxed a policeman out of the ring in the second round, and the fight was called a knockout. The Africa Foundation team was declared over-all winners and returned home victorious and jubilant. Simeon was particularly pleased because the game had proven him right. The children's tremendous physical energies had been put to good use.

That same week Simeon received a report that some of the older boys were still smoking dope. Moniko Farm where they lived was a tea plantation with coffee trees and a coffee factory. The boys were hiding among the coffee trees for their smoking sprees, so Simeon also hid among the trees and caught them red-handed. The boys boxed him and overpowered him. Simeon immediately stopped all boxing activities. The boys had turned their boxing skills against the sponsor.

Just as any other parents, we had to learn from our mistakes and profit from our experiences.

KAYANJA

Kayanja's father was not really a beggar, though he lived like one; he was a madman, exhibiting many obvious signs of mental illness. He carried his two sons wherever he went, the older one on his back and the younger one, Kayanja, on his shoulders. I first sighted Kayanja's father in 1979 in the slums along the Nakivubo Channel.

This man would make his rounds along Kampala Road, carrying his two sons. In the evenings, he would retire and find shelter on a veranda somewhere. He would gather some sticks to cook food in some old container that he had picked up during the day. He would feed the paltry meal to his children, and they would fall asleep, resting for another day of meaningless wandering.

I first met this man one afternoon in 1979 as I was traveling to Rohana to see the children. I was walking with my chief Tanzanian escort. We had learned early on that walking was far better than risking travel in a hired vehicle. The drivers' daredevil antics were enough to persuade anyone of the joys of walking. The rundown condition of the cars, the scarcity of spare parts, and the bald tires almost always guaranteed a breakdown. As we approached the Nakivubo Channel, we noticed a madman collecting dry leaves and paper and putting them on the dead body of a child. We stopped for a moment and watched this strange scenario for a moment. Others passing by seemed almost unconcerned, as they had become calloused to the heartaches of life.

We stayed at Rohana until four o'clock. As we were returning to the hotel, we reached the same spot where we had watched the madman. The dead body was now under the heap of leaves and papers. We looked on in shock as the man set the pile on fire. As we walked away, we cringed at the laughter of others who watched mockingly. The madman ignored their scorn, standing motionless and stern and watching the child's body go up in flames. Perhaps he was not the madman at all but the most serious-minded human around.

I saw this man almost two years later while I was addressing the city beggars near the old bus park. He was still carrying his two children. That day I had the chance to talk to him. I needed to establish some kind of rapport with him before broaching the important business that I had to present to him. I wanted him to surrender his children to me willingly and gratefully. I greeted him warmly and complimented him for something I had seen him do several years earlier. Unfortunately, he paid no attention to me, and my efforts were futile.

I met him another time just outside the defunct bookstore near Constitutional Square. The young son, Kayanja, seemed to recognize me, for I could read a hint of familiarity through his wary smile. I commented to the father that the two children must be too heavy to carry and that I would be happy to relieve him by carrying the younger one. He smartly answered in the vernacular, "*Enjovu teremererwa masanga gayo,*" "An elephant will never find its tusks heavy." He meant that his sons were as precious to him as tusks are to the elephant. In return, I told him with a smile, "You win."

Not long after our encounter, the man wandered into the workshop on Kampala Road that had been allocated for the beggars to use as their handicraft shop. He came in to beg for money for something to eat. I gave him a friendly greeting, and he recognized me this time. I reminded him of our conversation outside the bookshop. I said to him, "Now you are begging for money, but I begged to have your son." Amazingly, he bent and lowered his son from his shoulders. "You take him," he offered. I quickly pulled out a ten thousand note and said to him, "Take it."

We agreed that he was free to visit his son at Rohana any time, but that was the last I ever saw of him. Not many days after, a speeding car ran him down, and he and his other son were killed instantly. What a terrible shock it was to us!

Despite his rocky beginnings in life, Kayanja adjusted quickly to our loving family environment and performed well in school. He came to know Jesus Christ as his Savior and grew into a committed servant of God. He completed his studies at Westminster Bible College, Zana, and is now pastoring a church at Munyonyo. Truly he can say with the psalmist:

> He brought me up also out of an horrible pit, out of the miry clay, and set my feet upon a rock, and established my goings. And he hath put a new song in my mouth, even praise unto our God: many shall see it, and fear, and shall trust in the LORD. (Ps 40:3)

15

From the Dust

THE WEDDING

IT STARTED AS A simple idea. Richard Nsubuga, one of the very first children in the orphanage that was started at Kasubi, was to get married. The reception was to be held at the Lukumbi Farm, where he was already acting as assistant manager. Serving on the wedding committee were the children from the old home of Kijomanyi before my exile: James Bombo, Robert Mayanja, Katusabe James, Lakeri Kabibi, Peter Tumwesigye, and Mayanja. In addition, Gary Bajus and his wife, Mary, worked tirelessly preparing for the wedding.

Word got out that one of the former street children was planning a wedding, and the press became enthralled with the idea. Ugandan television producers, newspaper journalists, and cameramen of all sorts did not want to miss one aspect of the wedding. "It is a revolution!" one man shouted. "A *muyaye* affords a church wedding, only a dream to many of us!"

As the interest increased, Imperial Hotel offered us the use of their reception hall. The hall, used by the wealthiest and most prestigious people in our country, was packed to capacity for the reception. Among the wedding guests were government ministers and other high-ranking government officials, reporters, and many friends. The wedding was even televised live.

Soon after the wedding, Richard and his lovely bride, Susan, were on a plane headed for the United States of America, where Richard later earned a degree in business administration. He was then instrumental in opening doors for four other of our children to go to America to study: Jack Bamutte, Joseph Okello, Jasper Suuta, and John Katende. These, however, were not the only ones to be able to study abroad. Hudson Ayo, Francis Byekwaso, and David Oyola studied in America, and Kafero went to Bulgaria to study medicine.

On one of my trips to America, I was in a hotel in Louisiana with Francis Byekwaso and David Oyola. David wondered how, out of so many children, I had chosen him to go to America. Before I could answer him, he shared that he was equally amazed at God's election, that out of millions of people, God had accepted him into his kingdom as a son. Francis reminded me of the day I had gotten him from the market. He admitted that when I told the children that the world was bigger than the market, he had thought I was making an overstatement.

"What I have seen," he continued, "has shown me that the world is infinitely bigger than the market. When I went to church, I had the same problem. The preacher talked about the kingdom of God; to me the kingdom was so small, but now it grows bigger every day."

In 1984, Richard and Susan returned from the States. The pressmen were still interested in following the story of Richard and his wife. When asked about his future plans, his answer was, "I have come back to assist my daddy in his task of rehabilitating the displaced children."

The interview, broadcast on national radio, caught the attention of a government secretary. He contacted me and made an offer to Richard of an executive post in the Ministry of Industry. I communicated that offer to Richard and told him how proud I was of him that so many people were recognizing his achievements. I encouraged him to consider the position and let me know his decision.

When I returned home, Penina had a message for me from Richard. He was not interested in any government job or any big post. "These people are happy with me," he had told my wife, "but they don't know the struggle Daddy had to make me what I am. I will work for Daddy and assist him in his work. I will help in retrieving my brothers and sisters from the dust."

ALEX

It was a sultry night in July of 1985. After midnight, the children at Rohana heard someone trying to push open the gate to the compound. They sat silent and frightened. In those days, no one dared go out after dark. They waited until morning to open the gate and were surprised to find a starving child leaning against the wall. They brought him in and invited him to the breakfast table, an invitation he gladly accepted. Except for his bright eyes, the boy was totally covered in dust. Young Alex told his story at the table that first morning.

He came from a village about forty miles from Kampala. One day as he was playing sports at school, there was a sudden loud noise. The children thought it might have been thunder and feared that rain might spoil their game. But the noise grew louder and louder and nearer and nearer. They soon realized that rather than thunder the booming noise was gunshots. It was the deafening sound from heavy machine guns. Children, teachers, and villagers began running in all directions. The headmaster shouted, "Children, take cover!" But before he could oversee their protection, he was taken away at gunpoint.

Alex took off with the ball and began running toward his home. Hearing gunshots along the road, he took a shortcut down a narrow path. But when he arrived, he found the place quiet and deserted. He spied a dog shot dead and lying in the doorway of his home. The thatched kitchen was in ashes. Then Alex saw with horror his mother's dead body lying in the pit latrine. He shouted her name and ran toward her, only to discover his father's lifeless body as well, shot dead. Apparently, his parents had been caught in the crossfire of the National Liberation Army and the National Resistance Army.

Panic-stricken, Alex ran, not knowing where he was going. The entire village of Nakalasa was deserted. Alex continued running, walking, and occasionally sleeping along the way until he eventually got to Kampala. He joined other children in the city who had escaped the wrath of the gun. Just before Alex came to us, some of the children had been picked up by the police for fighting over a bone someone had found on a garbage pit near the bus park downtown. Alex had narrowly escaped being arrested with the others, and a sojourner had brought him to our gate. That week, the police released forty children to the custody of Africa Foundation. The Rohana Club was so congested that we took the forty children into my home.

One evening as I sat around the table with the new arrivals, I discussed with them what they wanted to do. All of them except Alex wanted to go to school and start a new life. After prayer, young Alex followed me to my bedroom. I turned around and saw him standing in the corridor. "I want to talk to you, Daddy," he pleaded, standing stiff and motionless. He insisted that he needed to speak to me in private.

"You see, Daddy," he explained, "I really do want to go to school, but right now I cannot. You may think I am rebellious, but I am not. I want to go to the bush and learn to use the gun to face the people who murdered—" At the memory of his deceased parents, Alex suddenly lost consciousness and collapsed into my arms. Consolation for this disturbed child was difficult, as he was in utter despair. The following day he disappeared from the home. I suspected that I knew what had happened to him.

As I considered the plight of young Alex, it became apparent to me that any regime that uses brutality, murder, and revenge as a political solution is, in effect, sharpening a sword against its own existence. Those who survived their brutality would certainly rise up against them, given the opportunity.

REUNIFICATION

Of course, people were thrilled to be reunited with their friends and relatives after the Liberation War. However, some reunifications took years to finally be accomplished. One morning I was shocked when I went to my office to find a group of ten soldiers waiting for me, all of them unfamiliar to me. Although I could not detect any signs of hostility, I was apprehensive about their presence. Camouflaging my fear, I greeted them and invited them into my office.

One of them, probably sensing my uneasiness, immediately reassured me that they had come not in hostility, but to express their gratitude to me. One by one they related how they had lost their families, had had their homes destroyed, and had thought they would never see their children again. Their children, however, had come under my care and had been preserved through the turmoil and rescued from the ravages of war. When they finished, I found myself speechless. I was overjoyed that God had allowed me to protect and nurture their children, and that now the families could be reunited.

Two of these soldiers asked if I could remember two young men who had come to my office with a two-year-old child and had claimed to have left their identity in the car. They had left and had never come back. They admitted to being those two men. They came that day in a car marked "President's Office." The father asked how he could repay me for looking after the child for five years, but my reply was that my Master tells me to give expecting nothing in return (Luke 6:35). They wanted to take the daughter immediately, but I cautioned them about the difficulties of reintegration. The girl needed to become used to them by their offering small gifts and inviting her to family functions. Reintegration must be gradual, and for this girl, it took three months.

Interestingly, on the day the girl, then seven years old, left the home, she told her parents, "You take me on condition I come to see my sisters and brothers every weekend." It was a gentleman's agreement, and for the next three weekends, they brought their daughter to the children's home.

These ten soldiers were not the only ones to ever appear at Rohana. One morning I heard shouts of joy outside my office window. The children were very excited about something. I got up to look out the window to see what could possibly be making them so exuberant. There by the gate I saw a uniformed soldier, standing tall and proud and holding a gun almost bigger than himself. As I looked closely, I realized that the soldier was none other than Alex himself! He looked victorious. I ran out to welcome him back and soon learned that he was coming from the front lines.

When the National Resistance Army took over in 1986, there were two ranks in the army, that of *afendi*, or general soldier, and that of commander. I told Alex that I would gladly put him in school, and then he could rejoin the army as a commander when he got his education. He returned to the barracks to obtain permission, and soon he enrolled in Namiryango College. After completing Senior Six, he decided not to rejoin the army but went on to study medicine at Makerere University, where he performed very well.

> He raiseth up the poor out of the dust, and lifteth up the beggar from the dunghill, to set them among princes, and to make them inherit the throne of glory: for the pillars of the earth are the LORD's, and he hath set the world upon them. (1 Sam 2:8)

16

Forgiveness from the Heart

THE STREET CHILDREN

ONE OF MY PRIORITIES was to structure our homes as family units rather than organizations or institutions. We endeavored to give the children that which society had denied them: parental care, Christ-centered love, and counseling. As a reflection of Christ's own love, we provided food, shelter, clothing, medical care, and education. As the children realized the love that was extended to them, they were then able to comprehend the love of their heavenly Father and respond with gratitude and a God-honoring life. Our primary goal and sole purpose for existence was to see the love of Christ working through us leading these precious souls to him. Nothing that was accomplished in the homes, on the streets, in the slums, or even in the government could be attributed to me or the Foundation or even the many committed workers who gave their all to serve with us in Africa. Philippians 2:13 explains, "For it is God which worketh in you both to will and to do of his good pleasure." Truly we give God the glory for all that has been accomplished in the lives of the Ugandans.

In the book of Zechariah, an angel came to Zerubbabel to encourage him to continue his work of rebuilding the temple. He gave him a vision to remind him that the work was not in his own strength, but that God was working through him. When Zerubbabel asked the angel to explain the vision, the angel answered, "This is the word of the LORD unto Zerubbabel, saying, Not by might, nor by power, but by my spirit, saith the LORD of hosts" (4:6). Just as Zerubbabel trusted God for the task and gave him the glory, we too were careful never to take credit for having wisdom, abilities, or strength that brought about changes in the lives and hearts of others. We were mere tools in the hands of the Skillful Craftsman.

The street children of the eighties were largely children whose families had been liquidated by Amin's henchmen. These were rich or very educated families whom Amin saw as a threat to his regime. He killed the cream of our nation, and these street children were their children. They were children who were endowed with sharp minds and many hidden talents. The truth about these children became evident as they went through the various stages of rehabilitation. As they gained a sense of normalcy to their lives, they were able to use their intelligence and to develop their talents.

Street children developed a complicated network, zoning the city into colonies with each colony being under the control of a different "tiger of the jungle." The older children provided protection to the younger ones, and the younger ones, in turn, rendered services to the older ones. A newcomer was always subjected to hard forms of initiation. Each gang demanded total allegiance, so a child could not belong to two camps. A new member of a group was required to surrender his identity, including his name, and to submit to the leader of the group. The leader, or tiger of the jungle, had absolute power.

Bayaye, as street urchins were called, even developed a language of their own, called *luyaye.* They coined words that they used as a ploy to avoid security forces. They could discuss their mischief openly without being understood by outsiders.

To the outsider, street children appeared disorderly, disorganized, untidy, undisciplined, and rebellious, but inside the group these children were orderly, highly organized with a strong sense of solidarity, highly disciplined, and obedient to their code of conduct. They willingly submitted to the laws of the gang and were subject to punishment if they misbehaved or deviated from the norms of the group.

Street children suffer from a sense of social and psychological rejection that results in low self-esteem. Their poor self-image causes them to assert themselves in negative ways to prove to the general public that "they are there." From the child's own perspective, street life is an effective and acceptable survival strategy, and a viable plan to overcome extreme urban poverty and to achieve a subsistent income on the street.

KABALAGALA (PANCAKE)

Geoffrey Serwadda was one of the children forced to go into the streets to survive. He came from Gomba in 1980, and after staying on the streets for some weeks, was invited by Stanley Rugumayo to come and join the children's home at Rohana.

Geoffrey's story was indeed a sad one. Amin's regime, with its murder and destruction of human lives and property, had brought out the worst in the people of Uganda. Envy, jealousy, and personal vendetta flourished. If a person was interested in another man's wife, house, or land, all he had to do was to fabricate any lie against the owner, and the owner would be exterminated without any recourse. Such was the case with Geoffrey's father. Someone had made false allegations against him to the members of Amin's deadly Research Bureau, and he was murdered in cold blood.

The soldier who had killed Geoffrey's father rewarded himself by befriending Geoffrey's mother. She was still a young woman and fell as an easy prey to the soldier. He eventually convinced her to run with him to Zaire as a deserter. When she left, she told Geoffrey and his sister, "My children, do not worry; I go to bring you *kabalagala* [pancakes]." She left them sitting on the veranda, and she never returned.

One time I was invited to a call-in radio program to discuss the plight of the street children and my work with them. I took Geoffrey with me to give first hand insight into the life of a street child. A lady called in who sounded intimidated by the presence of street children and said she was horrified by the insecurity caused by the little vagrants. Before I could respond to her, Geoffrey quickly spoke up, "Madam, you cook good smelling food for your children. That food sends out attractive smells to us children on the verandas, but if you continue to ignore our presence, don't think that your own children are safe." That kind of prediction must have sent out negative feelings to many otherwise good, stable families. However, his scenario clearly represented the mindset of the emotionally damaged children who needed desperately to be noticed and nurtured and would lash out at the heartless society that had denied them of their dignity and other basic needs.

Geoffrey attended school and in 1995 completed university training. I attended his graduation, not as his guardian, but as his father. I was proud of his success and proud to stand beside the man he had become.

Just before he completed his teacher's training, Geoffrey Serwadda called a meeting with the members of Africa Foundation and a number of other children from the homes, who had already obtained their teaching credentials. He had a serious proposal to present to us all.

"Daddy," he explained directly to me. "We know why you did not want to put a school on this campus. You wanted to reduce the level of stigmatization of us as street children, and you wanted to increase our level of integration into society by making us associate with children in different schools. Daddy, we have excelled in that. I want to report to you that many of us who have completed school and those of us who are still in school have earned the highest grades available. We do so well that not a single teacher dares to call us garbage or street urchins. Your idea of integration has worked very well.

"Now we want to propose that we build a school here. We will invite those children from outside to show them another 'touch.'" With the word *touch* the room erupted into laughter. They had to explain to me that *touch* was one of the *luyaye* words coined on the streets.

Serwadda continued, "Having our own school and inviting outsiders in will not undermine your idea of "social integration" but will promote it in another way.

I could not argue with his reasoning, and the following year, 1995, we began a school and named it after Mama Rookmaaker in recognition of her impact on my life, her assistance and generosity to the Ugandan children, and her work with orphans in South India. Serwadda became its first headmaster.

In 1997, Serwadda's mother returned to Uganda and found her daughter living in Gomba. The village residents remembered her, but her daughter had been too young when she left to remember anything about her mother. She was very excited, however, and brought her to see her brother Geoffrey at Seta, where he lived and worked at Rookmaaker School. She introduced her mother to Geoffrey, but he did not respond. After a long pause, he said, "There is nothing I remember about you as my mother! You left us when we were too small, but I do recall one thing. Do you remember what you said to us when you left?"

The woman hung her head and replied, "My children, forgive me. I left you on the veranda, and I said to you that I was going to buy you *kabalagala*, and I lied to you."

Geoffrey did not wait for her to complete the sentence. He jumped as if he were hypnotized. He clutched his mother's throat and almost strangled her to death. His sister panicked and shouted for help, and with two other women, pulled Geoffrey away from his mother.

To this day, Serwadda does not know what came over him that day. He was not normally a violent individual. There was something about that word *kabalagala* that detonated a strong hidden emotion. He had always told his close friends and his sister that he would never touch *kabalagala* in his life. He just said that he hated the sight of it. Evidently it had become a symbol of the mother's mysterious disappearance and had come to mean mysterious death to him.

The mother regained her strength. She deeply regretted the pain she had caused by running away with a murderer and abandoning her children. She was ashamed of her wicked behavior, but her regret could not change the pain that she had caused to her children.

It is easy for upright, cultured, successful citizens to clump all street children into one category and call them *bad*. Fortunately, our heavenly Father, who sees us just as we really are—sinful and defiled—does not immediately condemn us. As a matter of fact, when he looked upon us and saw our sinful condition, rather than despise us, he devised a plan whereby his precious Son, Jesus Christ, could take upon himself a fleshly body, live a perfectly holy life, and then suffer our punishment on the cross. The Father placed all the sins of humankind upon his Son, and Jesus paid the debt that we all rightfully owed. And then, as if that were not enough, he has sent his Holy Spirit to woo us to himself. In our sin, there is nothing in us capable of desiring God. Just as the street children were unable to imagine a better world, so we cannot see beyond our sin. It is God's Spirit Who convicts us and draws us to God.

Just as many of the children willingly followed me to Rohana Club to freely receive food, clothing, love, and education, so all we must do to freely partake in God's munificent love is to fully trust his offer and receive the gift of salvation. He makes us a new creation and begins building a new life in us.

> Therefore if any man be in Christ, he is a new creature: old things are passed away; behold, all things are become new. (2 Cor 5:17)

SEBANGA

The street children and orphans of the eighties were the victims of Amin's vicious reign and the resulting Liberation War. Although that time has passed, there are still many homeless and destitute children in Uganda. Some are the orphaned children of AIDS victims, but some are the casualties of a cruel, selfish, godless society. Many of the children willingly leave their tumultuous homes for a better life on the streets.

On August 7, 2000, both print and electronic media carried the story of Enock Sebanga, a child who had been tortured and almost starved to death by his own father and stepmother. Charles Kayongo, who lived with his family in Kalerwe about four miles outside of Kampala on Kampala-Gayaza Road, had intentionally withheld food from his son to weaken him. His plan was that as soon as the heavy rains came, he would throw Sebanga out to be swept away by the water channel. Fortunately for little Sabanga, his Aunt Regina Nabakooza had watched him suffer long enough and finally reported her brother and sister-in-law to the authorities for this abuse. The town security personnel went to Kayongo's house and found Sebanga lying almost dead in a pile of human feces under the bed. Kayongo and his wife were arrested, and little Sebanga was taken to the hospital in Mulago.

As soon as I heard the radio report, I rushed to Mulago to find Sebanga in very critical condition. I was horrified to find a boy whose ribs could clearly be counted. He had festering wounds all over his body and dry cracked lips. Poor Sebanga was just a dehydrated bundle of bones. A lady at his bedside commented, "This is just a picture of a human being reduced to absurdity." When I stretched out my hand to greet him, he weakly and hoarsely asked for water. It was a miracle of grace to hear a voice coming from these bones.

Sebanga's situation opened my eyes to the brutal child abuse some children endure. It was an extreme example of why some children would rather abandon their homes and live on the streets. My heart went out to this precious child, and I determined to provide some hope for him. I took some clothing, bedding, and food to him while he was in the hospital. I said to him that though he had been denied proper shelter, I would give him a house to live in, food to eat, clothes to wear, and an education.

Several days later, Sebanga's birth mother traveled all the way from Rakai to see him. She had left Sebanga with his father when he was only two years old, so he had no recollection of her. She introduced herself to her son, now almost ten years old. He responded to her with a stern voice, "You have come because you heard that I was given a house by Daddy Kefa. That is the only reason you are here." Shamed by her own child and remorseful for her irresponsible behavior, the mother quickly found a reason to leave the room. Not surprisingly, she never returned.

Kayongo and the stepmother were sentenced to sixteen years in prison. Sebanga's Auntie Regina later told me that her brother, Kayongo, had made Sebanga's mother pregnant while she was a young girl still in school. The father was afraid that it would be found out that he had been involved with a schoolgirl, and wanted to remove the evidence of the affair by getting rid of the child.

Sebanga was not the only child in our home who had been traumatized by his parents. We had at least ten others who were suffering emotionally from abuse by family members. We were not only able to provide for their physical and spiritual needs, but we also had the opportunity to provide trauma counseling from a group of Japanese social workers who had come to Uganda. Although they could not speak our language, they had a method of using facial and hand gestures to diagnose and treat the children to help them deal with the trauma. After about two months of working with the children, one of the counselors was able to speak our language well enough to communicate with me. He explained that if this type of trauma were not treated, it would surely manifest itself later in the victim's life. In one way or another, all victims of abuse will turn their hostilities onto society. He told me that if someone took the trouble to analyze Sebanga's father, he would find that somewhere in his background there had been trauma, brutality, or torture of some kind that had gone untreated.

Sebanga started going with me to church. During one service, I preached from the book of Philemon. Onesimus was a servant of Philemon who had cheated his master and had been sent to prison. In prison, the Apostle Paul had ministered to him, and the servant had been gloriously saved. Paul wrote to Philemon, pleading with him to forgive Onesimus. I pointed out in my sermon that church discipline was never intended to destroy believers, but to restore them to fellowship with God and the church. As we were driving home, Sebanga told me that he wanted to become a pastor. When I asked him why, he replied, "Because I see it is difficult to forgive." His remark was followed by silence. For almost an hour, he sat deep in thought, not making a sound. I could tell there was a serious struggle within his heart. Finally he broke the silence. "As a Christian, now I forgive my parents, and I give them to God, for he knows how to handle them."

> For if ye forgive men their trespasses, your heavenly Father will also forgive you: But if ye forgive not men their trespasses, neither will your Father forgive your trespasses. (Matt 6:14–15)

17

The Night Commuters

KONY

ALTHOUGH UGANDA HAS BEEN liberated from Idi Amin, one of the most notorious tyrants of all time, there continues to be political unrest throughout the country. The British controlled the country as a colony until 1962. Unfortunately they failed to train the Ugandan people to rule themselves and left them with no capable leaders in the government or the military. As a result, since their independence in 1962, there have been eight coups resulting in eight different presidents. Additionally, the country has been ransacked by various armies fighting for tribal dominance, political power, and self-gratification.

Obote was the first prime minister in 1962 and became president in 1966, but Idi Amin overthrew him in 1971. However, in 1980 Obote regained power but was ousted a second time in 1985 by his own army commander, Okello Lutwa. Lutwa was an Acholi, one of the two tribes of warriors in the country. The only other tribe of warriors was the Karamojong. Lutwa's was an army takeover, but fortunately it involved very little bloodshed. In the following year, the National Resistance Army, headed by Yoweri Museveni, forced out the Lutwan government, marking the eighth coup since Independence in 1962. After capturing most of the strategic positions in the southern part of the country, Museveni's forces began moving northward.

Now Museveni was neither Acholi nor Karamojong, but a Hermite, and the soldiers of the Uganda National Liberation Army (UNLA) and the Acholis were incensed that a Hermite would dare come against them with a gun. Captain Karama of the UNLA led a fierce resistance to Museveni's National Resistance Army (NRA). At Kaluma Bridge, Karama was killed, and his soldiers dispersed. As a result, the entire north came under the control of the NRA, and Museveni was in complete control of the country.

Another Acholi, a woman of great charisma called Lakwena, raised a large force of fighters from the Acholiland to fight against Museveni and the NRA. She called herself the Spirit, and would smear the fighters with certain herbs and convince them that their bodies were bulletproof. They had complete faith in her claims. A former minister of education who also believed in her powers later joined her. She galvanized a huge army, and before long, she had reached Bunya via eastern Uganda. Bunya was in Busoga, which was a stronghold of UPC (Obote's party). Many UPCs almost joined Lakwena, but when asked what manner of spirit she was, she denied that the spirit was either DP (the Catholics' party) or UPC; she was of a Lakwena spirit. She lost any support that she would have received in Busoga, and she made herself vulnerable to a miserable defeat. Having barely escaped capture by NRA forces, she abandoned her army and fled to Nairobi, Kenya.

In the same year, 1986, the remnants of Lakwena regrouped under the Lord's Resistance Army (LRA), led by Joseph Kony in the Acholiland. His new army title using the word *Lord* was just the beginning of his deceit and hypocrisy. Kony claimed to receive his power from the Gulu hills where the Acholi gods reside. He built altars there on which he sacrificed infants and used their blood to smear on his soldiers for their protection against bullets.

Kony had not been in control of the Lord's Resistance Army for long when the country was shocked to hear that over thirty girls had been abducted from the Aboke Girls' School and taken to be used as Kony's wives and as rewards for his commanders. It was believed that Kony himself had over fifty wives. Many of the girls, from thirteen to fifteen years of age, were used as sex objects: they were raped, defiled, or forced into sex. Because of this cruel sexual harassment, many of them were made pregnant, even by AIDS victims

The Catholic sisters who ran the girls' school went everywhere appealing for help in recovering and rescuing the abducted girls, but in vain; no one would help. Their cries for help were lost and forgotten like a lone voice in the wilderness. The world had heard nothing and was altogether ignoring the Kony atrocities.

More shocking stories began to emerge. Some girls who resisted abduction had their lips cut off, their ears removed, and their noses battered. Kony's brutality and violation of human rights reduced young girls to the most repugnant image anyone could imagine. The world looked on in total apathy as Kony defied every human right and social theory imaginable.

The abductions have continued for years. Children might be abducted for a day or two to carry loads of goods that the rebels stole from the villages they raided. Some abductees might be kept for several weeks before being released. Many boys and young men were forced to become soldiers and commit atrocities themselves. Many of the girls were forced to marry the soldiers or become prostitutes. And then there were the babies—

When in Parliament, I formed the Parliamentary Forum for Children. We worked closely with UNICEF and Save the Children's Fund in Uganda. Now I had the opportunity to travel to the north of Uganda with other agencies that were dealing with children. One time, we were in Kitgum in north central Uganda, and the government had just reiterated its offer of amnesty for rebels from Kony's army who wanted to surrender and return from the bush. President Museveni always emphasized amnesty to the rebels in his efforts to end the war. He believed that if the leaders (Kony in particular) were killed, then new leaders would rise up and carry on the tradition of killing; but if the leaders were granted amnesty in exchange for a promise of reformed ways, then the killing would stop.

Our parliamentary delegation met with one of Kony's commanders who had just returned from his army. His testimony shocked and terrified us as he told how he had been abducted and conscripted into Kony's army as a commander. Four of Kony's soldiers had taken him to the Sudan-Ugandan border to test him. The test was one of absolute cruelty. He had to tie a *Kandoya* of two victims, one male and one female, at different places. (A *Kandoya* is a human being tied with a rope until the entire body is twisted into one big ball.) Fearful of his own death, the abductee cooperated.

This soldier spotted a nearby herdsman, chased him down, caught him, and started kneading him until his muscles, head, and stomach were about to burst like a balloon. Then came the real test. The soldier was forced to take a hammer, smash the herdsman's head open, and drink all the brains without letting one drop fall to the ground. The recruiting officers were satisfied. Next they had to find a female victim to complete the test. They walked on.

"By this time," the man told us, "I did not know myself. The world was just turning around. I walked as if my feet were not touching the ground." He himself was a victim—a victim of something he never understood.

As they rounded a certain corner, the group saw a woman carrying a jar of water on her head, and the hunt began. The woman could not run very far. He soon captured her and began to tie her up in the *Kandoya* form. The soldier then chopped off her head and drank all of the blood without letting one drop fall to the ground. He had to undergo these two tests in order to qualify as a commander, a commander who would be loyal, obedient, and ruthless. The soldier testified that he was now the best "victim" to kill anything that appeared in his sight. He told us that his goal in the bush had been to kill his own father. As he told us this story, our entire delegation became terrified. His eyes began to bulge out and he said, "Even now I smell blood and am ready to kill." One of the Acholi elders told us that this man, as he had surrendered, was now ready to undergo the Acholi ritual of reconciliation. This ritual included stepping over an egg set along a walking stick and then eating a slain goat. This rite allows the victim to be readmitted into the Acholi community by absolving his sins, reconciling him with himself, and helping him realize his position in society.

Since 1978, Kony has been abducting people, especially children, whom he drags to his colonies to groom into Kony pawns. To them, Kony is an infallible giant. To him, they are a camp of enslaved dummies, who have no hope and cannot think for themselves. They are to him the "do-as-I-say, think-as-I-may-direct." A boy who was trying to escape from Kony's clutches was caught and taken to him. Kony told the boy, "If you were trying to escape, you surely have a brain tumor. Which one of my commanders will help you have it removed?" And the boy was then shot dead on the spot.

One of the charismatic pastors organized a team of believers who prayed and fasted for weeks before invading the Gulu Highlands where Kony's altars were. They returned with horrible revelations. They had managed to break down three of Kony's altars but had missed the fourth. At these altars infants had been sacrificed to the pagan gods, and their blood smeared on the bodies of the commanders for their protection and empowerment for victory against any impending foes.

Kony would claim any religion that would reinforce his magic spells. He would be Protestant today, Catholic tomorrow. He sought powers from Islam and Hinduism. Since his gods reside in the mountains, he has tried to climb Mount Elgon in order to communicate with them. Kony has never followed the biblical God, even from the inception of the Lord's Resistance Army.

In the North were established Internally Displaced People's Camps (IDPCs). These IDPCs were supposed to be safe harbors where people could live protected from Kony's atrocities, but in these camps adults and children are subjected to the most unhygienic conditions possible. Ironically, the safe harbors turned into the most vulnerable places for insecurity, disease, and abnormal human behavior. Out of these dreadful camps came the children who are often referred to as "night commuters." Children as young as three years old and as old as seventeen leave the camps every afternoon and walk as far as twelve miles to spend the nights in safety on the city streets of the larger towns. They sleep wherever they can find a spot—at bus parks, on verandas, in vacant buildings, under bridges. Then next morning they get up and walk the twelve miles back to their camp. All the people have been suffering from the many atrocities committed by a man who had no program but to murder and maim the people he was supposed to be protecting.

The founding members of the Parliamentary Forum for Children were heavily burdened about the contemptible circumstances for children in our country. We would meet once a week to pray about the appalling and ever-worsening conditions. We were concerned about the plight of the night commuters in the north, about the saddening levels of rape and child defilement, about the forced marriages for young girls, about the naked realities of HIV/AIDS, and about ritual killings of young children. The Forum wanted to see appropriate laws put into place to redress these detestable conditions. We wanted to see legislators becoming a voice for the voiceless children. We wanted to see a Parliament that would promote child-friendly laws and policies. There were those organizations in the north, such as World Vision, that were doing everything possible to provide relief from the suffering. They provided counseling to returning abductees—to traumatized children with deep psychological wounds, with shattered hopes and dreams, with futures that had been tampered with, trampled upon, and utterly destroyed by human greed and lust. Such a disturbance in God's creation is intolerable.

UNICEF invited some members of the Parliamentary Forum to fly to Gulu to assess the situation with child night commuters. I was stunned to find that despite the fact that millions of dollars had been deposited into accounts for the relief of these people, children still carried mats for blankets.

Evidently there was a problem with delivery of services and with products purchased. Resentment began to burn within me, though I could not point a finger at any source of this black spot of greed and dishonesty. I looked on with agony as I saw hundreds of these children walking barefoot, some with cracked feet. Some had torn school uniforms; many carried their books without a school bag. They were drenched by the rains and dirty from the dust. The small ones, poor kids, had unbrushed, matted hair. They all had dusty curls. None of them had Vaseline for their parched faces, and apparently bathing soap was a luxury that none could afford. I could tell from one child with torn pants that underwear was also a luxury they did without. As a person who has worked with homeless street children, I could read from their faces that some of these children had contracted gonorrhea or syphilis. Some children had ringworm spots on their heads.

I longed to be a business tycoon with money enough to purchase all the necessities that the children lacked. They needed such simple items as soap, shoes, school uniforms, school bags, hair brushes and combs, Vaseline, body lotions, socks, underwear, toothbrushes, toothpaste, pajamas, blankets, basic medicine, and worm medication.

I visited an IDPC establishment in Pabo, where there was a primary school, but the children there had no hope of getting any education beyond that. I talked to a boy there who was getting ready to take his Primary Leaving Exams (PLE) and asked him whether or not education had given him any sense of hope for the future. He replied, "I may pass these exams, but I have no future. I have nightmares of being abducted, tortured, or killed."

Then I tried one last question. "What are you living for?"

"I live a lifeless existence at best," he replied. I stood there speechless as the boy made the most shocking statement I have ever heard: "I fear human beings more than I fear animals."

The boy told me, "If you are going back to Gulu, I fear for you. When you see at a distance a human being trying to cross the road or peeping, run for your life, for that may be a trap for an ambush or a road mine."

I was surprised and responded with a question. "You fear for me?"

The boy replied, "I fear for anybody coming here from Kampala, because for us we have become numb against any bullet or death. Kony rebels have burned these houses you see here. They have been burned down three times. Sometimes you will see nothing but smoke and the people running in all directions. Mothers can come back crying and un-earth the dead bodies of their children burned in those thatched huts. We don't have anything here that is durable. All these houses you see here can disappear in a moment."

It was true. When my delegation reached Lacha Hospital, we found bodies that had sustained burns from another camp. Some had been burned to death. The boy was right, because in just a day's experience, we too had become numb.

That evening as we were having dinner in a restaurant, I asked one honorable woman of parliament whether she had any plans concerning what she had seen. Her reaction was, "I am afraid. When you have rubbed shoulders with a people without much hope, you also begin to question the validity of any hope for the unknown."

The United Nations indicted Kony to have him arrested for the atrocities he had committed against the people. The war in the north had affected everybody in Uganda. Not only were the innocent abducted, killed, robbed, and burned, but also many soldiers in the Uganda People's Defense Force (UPDF) had been killed, maimed, blown up in land mines, and tortured horribly for their resistance. But the rebels in the LRA were so ruthless and demonic that it was impossible to capture them or control them in any way.

Amin's reign of terror, state-inspired brutality, and years of mass murder had left a negative legacy to the people of Uganda. After Alube's attack on his life in 1972, Amin had turned all of his fury and wrath to-ward the Acholi. At the time of his fall in 1979, Amin was believed to have killed over 500,000 people, leaving behind over 300,000 widows and 800,000 orphans. A good number of these widows were Acholis. Then, just seven years later, Kony began killing and torturing the Acholis—his own people. The level of absolute poverty in Uganda has been around 35 percent in the past, but in northern Uganda, it is twice that rate. The war there has denied anyone in that region any sense of tomorrow. The people there live such unstable, horror-filled lives that they do not even know what it means to plan for the future or even to have confidence in being sustained for today. The concepts of "tomorrow" and "next week" and "next year" can be conceived only in an environment of peace and stability.

In July of 2006, peace talks began between the LRA and the Ugandan government. The talks, headed by the vice president of Sudan, Riek Machar, took place in Juba, Sudan. The people of the southwestern regions of Sudan were especially interested in a peace agreement with the LRA in order to rid themselves of the ravages of the group, who had been taking their terrorism across the borders of Uganda. In October of 2006, the country of Uganda, as well as many of the countries of the world community, was relieved to hear that the peace talks had effected an agreed cease-fire. The terms of the agreement granted amnesty and safety to the LRA soldiers, and in return the soldiers promised to leave the general areas of Uganda and Sudan, and to gather in special areas provided for them. Kony's soldiers started gathering into two camps in Sudan and one camp in Uganda. There remains some haggling about all the specific terms of the agreement, but for the time being, the LRA rebels are not on the rampage.

Though the International Criminal Court from the UN had insisted on having Kony arrested for trial, President Museveni has retained his belief in the effectiveness of amnesty. Civil rights groups around the world have condemned the leniency granted to the LRA and have accused the government leaders of using the situation as a stratagem to gain the approval of the populace, but the agreement was favored by the majority of the people in northern Uganda.

In postcolonial Africa (after British rule) there have been more wars than ever before, and the continent has lived under political tension. In any form of decolonization, it may be simpler to decolonize the colonizer than the colonized. This distinction is comparable to dealing with the deceiver rather than the deceived, because the deceiver is very well aware of deceptive tactics. In any form of political upheaval, the leaders in Africa have been used as Ping-Pong balls.

Some time ago I read Tony Blair's African Commission report, *Our Common Interest*.[1] This document poses the question, why is Africa poor?, and concludes that Africa's poverty is planned. I will not hesitate to add that Africa's wars are equally planned. So long as these wars are played on

1. Commission for Africa. *Our Common Interest: Report of the Commission for Africa* (London: Commission for Africa, 2005).

the land of Africa, the Africans will never realize their potential and they will continue depending on foreign aid. They will continue to beg from the parish club.

I remember a conversation I had in 1995 with a pastor from South Korea. This elderly man predicted that in fifteen years there would be a new scramble for Africa. Africa is replete with minerals that are practically untouched. It has underground oil, forests, fresh water, and wildlife. These valuable resources attract the wealthier nations, which are looking for new sources of products and business. They come into the country and treat the people well, win their friendship, and then take advantage of their gullibility. This scramble has already begun, and the questions remain: Whom will this quest profit? Who are the beneficiaries? Will the African poor benefit, or are they to be washed off the shores of the Indian Ocean, or will they be forced to swim upstream? The rich will sail through the storm of postcolonialism.

OWNERS OR MESSENGERS?

In November 2006 I was guest speaker at Taylor University during their World Opportunities Week, which was designed to increase Taylor students' involvement in global missions through prayer and active service. This was a highly commendable program for any university today in the history of America. The enthusiasm by which I was received cheered my heart with humility. I thanked God for the university's leadership. I had the joy of meeting and working with the co-directors, young people Andrew Ulasich and Valerie Schmidt, and I also had the privilege of meeting the president of the university, Dr. Eugene Habecker.

The theme of the week was taken from Genesis 12:1–2, speaking of God's blessings to the nations through Abraham. As I prayed through this text, I had to look beyond all the materials I collected from the commentaries and listen to God, and slowly the text began to unfold. The more I waited upon God in prayer, the more God filled my heart with an overriding timeless message.

God's blessings to Abraham made Abraham the instrument and not the owner of those blessings. God remained the owner, and Abraham became the messenger. God's blessings to Abraham made Abraham a steward, for indeed the beneficiary was not Abraham, but the nations. And Abraham was to give an account to God of how these blessings benefited the beneficiaries, the nations of the earth. No wonder that when Isaac blessed Jacob, he passed on the blessings to his son that God had given to his father, Abraham: "And God Almighty bless thee, and make thee fruitful, and multiply thee, that thou mayest be a multitude of people; And give thee the blessing of Abraham, to thee, and to thy seed with thee; that thou mayest inherit the land wherein thou art a stranger, which God gave unto Abraham" (Gen 28:3 -4). To Abraham, Isaac, and Jacob, that blessing was more than a promise of material wealth and power. It was more than a promise of land, of freedom, and of family. It was the promise of the Savior who would redeem the world from their sins. Jacob understood the magnitude of that promise. When he was dying, he blessed each of his sons, and his blessing of Judah revealed that the promised Messiah would come through Judah's line: "The sceptre shall not depart from Judah, nor a lawgiver from between his feet, until Shiloh come; and unto him shall the gathering of the people be" (Gen 49:10). According to Matthew Henry, the word *Shiloh* means "that peaceable or prosperous one," and refers to the Savior.[2] From the tribe of Judah came King David, and finally in God's perfect timing came the Lord Jesus Christ, God incarnate, to redeem sinful humanity.

How wonderful that that promise was not only for the Jewish nation as the bodily descendants of Abraham, but that it was passed on to the Gentiles—that we too might be partakers in the blessings and riches of God's grace! The Apostle Paul explains in Galatians 3:14, "Christ hath redeemed us from the curse of the law, being made a curse for us: for it is written, Cursed is every one that hangeth on a tree: That the blessing of Abraham might come on the Gentiles through Jesus Christ; that we might receive the promise of the Spirit through faith." It was God's blessing to Abraham that came to the Gentiles through Christ our Lord. Now as we have become the beneficiaries of God's promise, we must also become the messengers. As God's faithful servants from the past have preserved the message and passed it on to us, so it becomes our responsibility to share the truth with others. We must not be satisfied to be the owner of the blessing, but we must be determined to be the instrument to bring that blessing to the lost and dying. We must take the light of God's Word to the dark corners of the world. We must share with the world the love of Christ, and point them to the ultimate solution to all their problems. As

2. Henry, Matthew. *Matthew Henry's Concise Commentary on the Whole Bible* (Nashville: Thomas Nelson, 1997), 71.

souls are groping in the darkness of sin, are we sitting complacently in the sunshine of his love, ignoring their needs?

As a people called of God, we cannot hide our heads in the sand and remain impervious to human suffering caused throughout the nations by the evil one.

My heart was blessed to know that the video *Invisible Children* exposed Kony's atrocities against the children, the night commuters in northern Uganda.[3] The American people saw the problem and responded with compassion. People, especially the youth, took to the streets in many cities in America and demonstrated their concern for the suffering children in Uganda. The demonstrators walked miles on the streets of their cities and then slept in parking lots before walking back to their original meeting places the following morning. They wanted to understand, to some extent, the plight of the night commuters, and also they wished to make others aware of the suffering in Uganda. This response is historic, and I say bravo to the young American population who are sowing seeds of international reconciliation, restoring the image of Puritan America, and answering Africa's long cry for America's friendly foreign policy toward African countries.

However, foreign policy, government intervention, sympathy, and charity are not enough. All people everywhere need to be changed on the inside; they need to become new creatures through Christ Jesus. They need to be born into God's family by his saving power. As men and women experience the new birth and begin to grow in the Christian faith, they will realize the hope that is in Christ. As they are set free from the bonds of the evil one, they will have victory over sin. Through salvation, people become heirs of God. Is there any greater gift that we could share than the gift of eternal life?

> But when the fulness of the time was come, God sent forth his Son, made of a woman, made under the law, To redeem them that were under the law, that we might receive the adoption of sons. And because ye are sons, God hath sent forth the Spirit of his Son into your hearts, crying, Abba, Father. Wherefore thou art no more a servant, but a son; and if a son, then an heir of God through Christ. (Gal 4:4–7)

3. Jason Russell, Bobby Bailey, and Laren Poole, in association with People Like You. *Invisible Children: Rough Cut*, DVD (directed by Jason Russell, Bobby Bailey, and Laren Poole. Invisible Children, 2006).

18

The Fishing Nets

IN THE ELECTIONS OF 2001, I won the Ntenjeru South seat in parliament with an overwhelming majority. My constituency comprised parts of two counties, Nazigo and Kangulumira. In Nazigo, there was a remote village named Kasega that bordered the Nile River. This was a very poor village without a school, a shop, or a church. Most of the women in this village were exceptionally tiny and had very tiny children whom I thought to be sick.

Whenever I campaigned in this village, the voters would stand along the road with their hands in the air shouting, "Our man! Our man!" Although I enjoyed my popularity in this village, I had the feeling that something was amiss in this place. After I was elected, I passed through this village and was greeted with deafening songs of victory. The women shook banana leaves in the air and with them formed a green canopy over my head against the sunset.

It was around this time that a retired senior staff member of Safe Harbor, Edwin Cornwell, came to Uganda with a team of mission volunteers from Nevada. Safe Harbor is a Christian international relief organization out of California that ministers to societies that are suffering from fear, hopelessness, persecution, or a natural disaster. They take the good news of God's saving grace to the suffering people; they also minister to the physical needs of the people. When I first met Eddie, I shared with him my concerns for the health of the people in Kasega. I asked if the doctors on his team would visit the village. He readily agreed, and we left immediately for Kasega.

When we arrived in the village, we found literally hundreds of people waiting to receive the visitors from America. They had arranged a place under a huge mango tree to receive their American guests. After the ritual greetings and songs, the women and children were separated to be examined by a doctor. The village elders invited Eddie to go into their "reception room," a small hut designated for a conference. I entered first to find more than fifteen elders waiting to share the village's needs. Eddie bowed like a Chinese elder to enter the hut. Some elders quickly noticed that the *mzungu* (white man) was uneasy. The elder in charge told some of the other elders to move out of the hut, but the crowd outside was almost pushing the hut down, and it was impossible for the elders to leave. It took over twenty minutes of pushing, yelling, bargaining, and pleading to gain order in the place.

When the meeting finally began, a report was handed to Eddie. The main request was for help in acquiring fishnets since the majority of the residents were fishermen. Eddie readily agreed to get the nets. The quicker he could get out of the turmoil the better.

Eddie's contact person in Uganda and the driver for the day, Rashid Luswe, drove right into the middle of the crowd to pick us up from the conference. He then drove us over to the area where the women and children were being examined. There the doctor informed us that the women were not sick, but that they and the children were severely malnourished. The doctor had observed that the people in the area were growing millet. He advised the adults to mix millet with milk and to give the mixture to the children, and to eat it themselves. He pointed out that with the fish from the Nile, there was no reason for malnutrition. The people just lacked the knowledge of what foods their bodies needed to maintain good health. As we were rode off in a cloud of dust, we could see hundreds of hands waving goodbye to the American visitors. In less than three months, there were visible signs of recovery. The women looked well, and the children's cheeks had filled out nicely. Their faces had begun to glow with radiant health.

Eddie and the team returned to Nevada, and Eddie set out to locate and purchase the fishing nets. Several weeks later, I went back to Kasega and was greeted with various expressions like," Kefa, what did you do for us? What did you do to get an American to hug me?" The people from Nevada had not only allowed their hearts to be touched by the immense poverty of the people of Kasega, but they had allowed their bodies to be touched by the people as well. The Americans had even reached out to hug the villagers to show their love and compassion. The rural peasants were thrilled at the experience of being hugged, an experience they had never enjoyed in their lives. A touch of love from an American was more valuable to them than anything in the world.

Apparently the Americans understood the biblical concept that God has created all, the rich as well as the poor, and that they coexist under the canopy of his love. Proverbs 22:2 teaches us that "The rich and poor meet together: the LORD is the maker of them all." The Safe Harbor volunteers were operating under the principles of Psalm 82:3–5: "Defend the poor and fatherless: do justice to the afflicted and needy. Deliver the poor and needy: rid them out of the hand of the wicked. They know not, neither will they understand; they walk on in darkness: all the foundations of the earth are out of course." Truly the foundations for these people were "out of course," but someone had responded to their needs and was there to compassionately and self-sacrificially render help.

Eddie had taken a piece of dirty fishing net as a sample, but he could not get that size net in America. He tried to find the right size in London, but it was not there either. Finally, he located the exact size of net in Dubai. When the nets were ready for delivery, Eddie himself returned to Uganda to personally deliver them. I went to Entebbe airport to pick him up and was greeted by his beaming smile and glimmering eyes. His whole face glowed with excitement as he thrilled over the hope he was bringing to the people of Kasega. He had bought piles and piles of fishing nets, and eagerly shared with me the whole story of how he had found the perfect nets. We were both filled with excitement for the new opportunities being made available to the villagers, so we hurried to Kasega with the nets. As usual there was a huge gathering under a mango tree. Rashid toiled away unloading the rare nets. The women and children made much hullabaloo.

Now, Eddie never gave out anything for free, be it a donation or a grant, for he wanted people to appreciate what they received. He did not charge them money to make a profit or even to reimburse himself or Safe Harbor. He wanted the people to experience the pride of providing for themselves and not just living for handouts, and he wanted them to appreciate the value of what they received. In a short while, a group of elders announced to Eddie that the nets he had brought were not the right size. Upon this pronouncement, Eddie's blood pressure shot up. He was furious. Of course they were the right size! They were exactly the size of the sample he had been given! Seeing his anger, I gently pulled him away from the crowd. We walked a good distance from the people to allow him to cool down. When we finally returned to the vehicle, we discovered that all the nets were gone.

"Where are the nets?" Eddie inquired angrily.

"They have taken them all," replied Rashid.

Eddie was shocked beyond words that the Africans were so offensive as to criticize the nets and then actually steal them.

Eddie then turned to me. "Are these the people you represent in parliament?"

I made no comment.

We drove over thirty miles to Mukono, and Eddie was so upset that he did not speak a word to me the entire way. When we came to Mukono Town near the Christian University, he finally said to Rashid, "Don't you think the reverend wants to go home?" Rashid and I both understood the message. I took a taxi to my house.

A day before he left Uganda, Eddie phoned me and invited me to his hotel. I reached Equatorial Hotel and found that he was not in his best mood. He served me hot tea and asked me the same question. "You still represent your people of Kasega in parliament?" By this time I was so confused. I found myself saying to him, "Eddie, they are my people and their culture is so different from a white American's. When they said, "These are not the right size," they were in fact saying to you, "Lower the price or give us these nets at no cost."

Eddie gave a disgusted laugh. He did not accept my explanation for the reprehensible behavior of the villagers. He called one of his sons and asked him, "Did the reverend come in a taxi or his own car?" Again I got the message. I left the hotel and said to myself, "This man has really ruined my morning."

That day I was so upset that I did not even go to parliament. In less than two weeks, I received a long distance telephone call. I could hardly believe my ears. It was Eddie, and he was apologizing for his attitude and behavior. He then confessed that God had impressed upon his heart not to allow cultural differences to become barriers to his mission. In our conversation, Eddie convinced me that the real barrier was not a cultural one but the absence of the gospel in the lives of the people of Kasega. I realized that he was right. The people were wrong in the way they had treated him, but we both came to the realization that the core problem was that they were sinners and needed salvation. They needed the gospel to make them into new creations and to instill in them a true sense of morality.

He told me that he was coming with another team from Nevada to build a church at Kasega. He would share the gospel with the villagers and would give them the opportunity to have their lives changed by the power of God. That church would then act as a point of contact between the two cultures of America and Africa. Today in Kasega, there is a vibrant church, a medical clinic, and a school. The people of Kasega are growing spiritually and, as a result, are enjoying physical development and economic growth with their fishing and farming industries.

My interaction with Edwin Cornwell gave me a tremendous challenge. I started asking myself whether I had done anything through the power of the gospel to make a difference in my home county of Ntenjeru. There are neighboring villages of Kawuna, Sayi, Kituuza, Naluwala, Mpumu, Salaama, Mpata, Bugolombe, Bugigi, Kisoga, and Kiyoola that have never heard the name of Jesus Christ and that must be reached with the gospel. If I don't tell them, who will? I can say as the Apostle Paul said, "Yea, so have I strived to preach the gospel, not where Christ was named, lest I should build upon another man's foundation" (Rom15:20).

My wife and I are presently in the middle of a move to Ntenjeru. Living in the village will enable me to preach the gospel to people who have never heard of the saving grace of Jesus Christ. We will be able to make the power of the gospel visible in such places. I will be using what I have come to call *Cornwell's method*, that is, using the gospel to build the moral fabric of the people before introducing developmental skills. I have learned that spiritual blindness is deadly.

> This I say therefore, and testify in the Lord, that ye henceforth walk not as other Gentiles walk, in the vanity of their mind, Having the understanding darkened, being alienated from the life of God through the ignorance that is in them, because of the blindness of their heart. (Eph 4:17–18)

During my 2006 visit to America, I spent a few days in Michigan. I enjoyed a visit with my friend Jasper Suuta, a longtime member of the first Presbyterian Church in Uganda, who now resides in Grand Rapids. As he was taking me to the airport, we made a stop at the Resurrection Life Church. The associate pastor, David Christian, showed us around the church grounds. I was greatly impressed. As a matter of fact, I almost missed my plane because I was so intrigued with all he had to share about his ministry. That church sharpened my vision and deepened my determination for the Ntenjeru Presbyterian Church. I had already chosen a five-acre parcel of land to build the church, but I was now inoculated with a new enthusiasm for the project.

Jasper shared my vision with Stanley Rugumayo, who serves the Lord in Washington, D.C. Stanley then called me several days later while I was in Panama City, Florida. He said to me, "Reverend, as founder of the Reformed Faith in Uganda, that church will be built in your honor, and I am contributing all the musical instruments for the 'Presbyterian Vibrations.'"

How thrilled I was that God was already providing for the new ministry! Someone has wisely said, "Where God guides, he provides." I was seeing God work out his precious plan of sharing the gospel throughout the world just by my willingness to follow his leading. Pray for the salvation of the people of Ntenjeru and for the work of the new church there.

19

The Mustard Seed

Another parable put he forth unto them, saying, The kingdom of
heaven is like to a grain of mustard seed, which a man took, and
sowed in his field: Which indeed is the least of all seeds: but when
it is grown, it is the greatest among herbs, and becometh a tree, so
that the birds of the air come and lodge in the branches thereof.
(Matt 13:31–32)

LIKE THE MUSTARD PLANT that comes from a tiny seed, the Presbyterian
Church in Uganda grew out of a small discipleship group of five. As
of 2006, there are now over 120 congregations in the country and three
presbyteries, one in the west, one in the east, and one in the central part
of the country. There will soon be one in the north, and we have a vibrant
General Assembly. Westminster Bible College was begun at Zana by the
persistent efforts of Emma Kiwanuka, and not far from there at Lubowa
is the African Bible College, the first of its kind in Uganda. The college
was started by one of my former professors at Westminster Seminary,
Professor Palmer Robertson. He is there today sharing the treasures of
God's truth with needy African souls.

What is Africa Foundation today began as an outreach of the dea-
cons of the First Presbyterian Church, Kampala—the church I started
when I first returned to Uganda in 1979. As the Foundation reached
out to the helpless children, widows, and beggars of our ravaged land,
lives were changed one by one, souls came to know Christ as Savior, and
young people were nurtured into becoming prosperous citizens. Many of
the children that we cared for are now serving God in our country and
abroad, working in the business world, and rearing families of their own.
Charles Kirigwajjo is now secretary of Africa Foundation—UK Chapter.
Sebugwawo is editor of the *Times* in Rwanda. Peter Yawe is a businessman

in Capetown, South Africa. Aziz is serving as one of the top officials of OPEC. Kafero is a doctor in Norway. David Oyola is a computer wizard in Seattle. Jasper Suuta and his wife, Suzan, are living in an exclusive community in a luxurious house that they built on their own in Grand Rapids, Michigan. Baker Katende is pastoring a large church in Boston. The list of success stories is too long to cover.

Many American ministers have helped the Presbyterian Church in Uganda to expand. Henry Krabbendam and Dan Herron pioneered the West Presbytery. Pete Anderson, a fellow alumnus of Westminster Seminary, who pastors a big church in Hawaii, has come to Uganda every year for the last six years and has built a different church every year. Brian Cross of New Calvary Church in North Carolina, along with members of his congregation, sponsored a church at Nkokonjeru and made substantial contributions to the orphanage at Dandira. Pastor Martin Phillips from California built the church at Luwero and has also contributed to our children's homes.

Churches in America or individuals coming to Uganda are free to choose a church that they wish to assist, and their money goes directly to that congregation. Dr. Henry Krabbendam is working on the same basis. Volunteers coming to Uganda are free to associate with any church of their choice. Volunteers from different churches in America, and short-term missionaries like Tony Carto, have played a big role in the advancement of the Reformed churches in Mbale, and we hope they will continue that legacy.

Much work has been done, however, by the indigenous pastors and evangelists. Edward Kasaija, one of the founding members of Africa Foundation, pastors the First Presbyterian Church, Kampala. Morris Oginga is a key pastor in the Eastern Presbytery churches, and Edward Isingoma is a pastor in Hoima.

VOICE OF THE VOICELESS

In 1999, the government mandated the formation of the National Council for Children to coordinate, monitor, and evaluate children for protection, survival, and development. The council was set up as a body through which the needs and problems of children could be communicated to the government and other decision-making institutions and agencies in Uganda. I was appointed chairman of that committee. By virtue of this position, I also became chairman of the Early Childhood Development Committee. In both of these positions, I headed committees composed of very powerful and resourceful members. We became very instrumental in advocating children's rights, lowering the high stunting levels, and reducing the high infant mortality rates. We also were able to increase immunization against infant diseases. Ugandans have had an aversion to immunizations of any kind because they were unfamiliar with the practice and were superstitious about the possible ramifications. Even today there are many, many children whose parents will not allow immunizations.

Ugandan president Yoweri Museveni was very supportive of these programs. He worked with us to expose the dangers of the HIV/AIDS pandemic, and introduced universal primary education. In less than a year, the number of primary-school children increased from 2.7 million to over 6 million. A slogan developed: "If a parent or guardian wants to violate your right to education, say, 'No, don't interfere with my future.'"

As chairman of the National Council for Children, I took the opportunity to explain to the committee that we could not ignore the various contributions of the different NGOs (nongovernmental organizations) as efforts to alleviate the escalating problem of street children. At the same time, we would be naïve if we failed to see that some of the methods employed by some of these NGOs have tended to attract more children to the streets. This has created the impression that some NGOs are operating as magnets to attract more and more children to the streets.

As a member of parliament representing the people of Ntenjeru South, Kayunga District, I was greatly encouraged by fellow parliamentarians to start a parliamentary forum for children. The seventh parliament started the forum with support from UNICEF and Save the Children Fund, Uganda. A children's office was opened in the parliamentary buildings, where children can register their concerns for the attention of the legislators.

I personally experienced no serious dichotomy between being a Christian, on the one hand, and being in politics and fighting for the cause of needy children, on the other hand. I threw myself wholeheartedly into these endeavors. My path was clearly correlated in my mind, and the tasks harmonized beautifully with one another. In my life, I am professionally an artist and a trained art historian, but I made sure that I did not fall behind in any of the challenges that God called me to pursue. My calling is actually a single task, namely, to let the power of God work through me to build the kingdom of God, not counting on my natural ability, but allowing God's grace to be manifest in my life.

> I am crucified with Christ: nevertheless I live; yet not I, but Christ liveth in me: and the life which I now live in the flesh I live by the faith of the Son of God, who loved me, and gave himself for me. (Gal 2:20).

> But by the grace of God I am what I am: and his grace which was bestowed upon me was not in vain; but I laboured more abundantly than they all: yet not I, but the grace of God which was with me. (1 Cor 15:10)

SECULARIZED VIEW

There are people who believe that we live in an impersonal universe that belongs to nobody. This idea is not a view of the African mind. A Jewish man from Florida made an interesting observation during his two-week visit to Uganda. He noticed at the kiosk of an herbalist that a medicine man would spit on the medicine before giving it to a patient. He wanted to know why he would do such a thing. I explained to him that in Africa a medicine man knows very well that this world belongs to someone. Spitting on the medicine may not be the most hygienic practice, but it is in recognition of the gods. Treating a patient is a spiritual activity in a world that belongs to the Creator God.

When I was at Westminster Seminary, Cornelius Van Til was my apologetics professor. He had actually retired but was still teaching some courses. He would invite us to his house for fellowship and biblical discussions. On one such visit, he showed us an orange tree he had planted in his backyard right along the property line between his house and his unsaved neighbor's house. He explained that he wanted his neighbor to have the opportunity to eat from the tree. He used the tree as a demonstration to us that he and his non-Christian neighbor did not really eat the same orange. The unbeliever eats an orange that he believes to be produced by chance, but the Christian eats an orange created by God. This principle is a departure from a secularized worldview that regards this world as an impersonal universe.

Chapter seventeen of Acts was Van Til's favorite biblical chapter, and he used to emphasize the passage in which Paul is preaching to the Greek philosophers. The Epicureans and the Stoics inquired as to what babble he was preaching; and Paul, starting from their apostasy, pointed them to the true and living God. He used a statue to "the unknown god" as a springboard to introduce the unbelievers to the true and living God. Would that our early missionaries had used the same approach with us. If they had taken the time to study the African worldview instead of dismissing it as worthless, they might have made a greater impact on our beliefs.

I truly believe that our task as Christians in Uganda is to lead the people to Christ as Paul did in Athens. Perhaps the day of the missionary is quickly passing. There are many indigenous Christians already in the country. We understand the ways of our people; we understand their background; we understand their worldview. We can start from that knowledge and draw them to the "unknown God." In order to reach these millions with the gospel, we must continue to love them; we must continue to minister to their needs; and we must speak out and tell them the good news that Jesus wants to be their Savior. He wants to cleanse them from the filth of sin and to give them new life in Christ.

We cannot, however, do the job alone. We need continued assistance from around the world. We need new ideas, financial assistance, builders, and workers. Perhaps you can help. Willing hands are always appreciated. Someone in a church I was visiting in America asked me once, "What could I do if I went to Uganda?" I asked him in return, "Can you put your arm around a motherless child and tell him that you care?" A man in a church playing the guitar was considering coming to Uganda to help in the work. I asked him, "How many guitars can you bring to Uganda?" A person can come to Uganda and share music with us. Another person can help replace a roof. Another person can share with us what Jesus has done for him. A group can bring Bibles or gospel tracts and distribute them. Young people can come play with our children and then share the gospel with them. There is no limit to the opportunities for ministry in our country.

Maybe you cannot come to Uganda, but you can pray. You can intercede before the throne of God for the people of Uganda. Pray for our leaders, for our government, and for our army. Pray for the safety of our people. Pray for our families. Pray for our children. Pray that the gospel will go forth and that through the power of the Holy Spirit, many people will come to faith in Christ. For it is only as men and women, boys and girls are born into the family of God and become new creations that true peace will come to Uganda.

And whosoever shall give to drink unto one of these little ones a cup of cold water only in the name of a disciple, verily I say unto you, he shall in no wise lose his reward. (Matt 10:42)

Illustrations

The Baby Department built at Dandira, Mokono, in 1986.

These children are washing at a borehole (well) provided by Christians from Texas. The girl on the handle is Samalie. She eventually went to Germany, studied German, and became a translator for Drite Welt Kries, an organization that renders assistance to Africa Foundation.

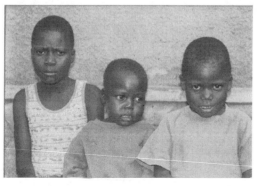

In Uganda, there are many families without parents at all. The oldest child becomes the leader of the family. This is one child-led family that came to Rohana.

Daddy playing with Moses, a child found on a garbage pit.

Daddy having lunch with the children.

Museveni made hats the latest fashion craze, and I decided to be in vogue.

Richard and Suzan Nsubuga with their children, Isaac, Faith, Rose and Derek. Richard was the muyaye who had the big wedding at the Imperial Hotel.

Daddy with Sebanga (right) and Sebanga's best friend, Semanda. Semanda was critically burned by his uncle and found on the road where he had crawled to escape the uncle's torture. A stranger paid bus fair for the boy and all others on the bus who were so repulsed by his smell and condition that they refused to ride if he was on the bus. The stranger brought the boy to Rohana Club, and we then took him to the hospital for treatment.